P9-DMF-224

BOOKS BY DANIEL J. BOORSTIN

The Exploring Spirit:
America and the World, Then and Now

* * *

The Americans: The Colonial Experience
The Americans: The National Experience
The Americans: The Democratic Experience

* * *

The Mysterious Science of the Law
The Lost World of Thomas Jefferson
The Genius of American Politics
America and the Image of Europe
The Image: A Guide to Pseudo-Events in America
The Decline of Radicalism
The Sociology of the Absurd
Democracy and Its Discontents
Portraits from the Americans
The Chicago History of
American Civilization (27 vols.; editor)
An American Primer (editor)
American Civilization (editor)

* * *

for young readers
The Landmark History of the American People
Vol. I: From Plymouth to Appomattox
Vol. II: From Appomattox to the Moon

THE EXPLORING SPIRIT

AMERICA AND THE WORLD, THEN AND NOW

THE
EXPLORING
SPIRIT

AMERICA AND THE WORLD,

THEN AND NOW

DANIEL J. BOORSTIN

RANDOM HOUSE   NEW YORK

First American Edition

Copyright © 1975, 1976 by Daniel J. Boorstin

All rights reserved under International and Pan-American Copyright
Conventions. Published in the United States by Random House, Inc.,
New York, and simultaneously in Canada by Random House of Canada
Limited, Toronto.
Originally published in a slightly different form in *The Listener,* a British
Broadcasting Corporation publication.

Library of Congress Cataloging in Publication Data
Boorstin, Daniel Joseph, 1914–
The exploring spirit.
1. National characteristics, American.
2. United States—Civilization. 3. Technology
and civilization. I. Title.
E169.1.B7516   1976   973   75–40553
ISBN 0–394–40602–8

Manufactured in the United States of America
2   4   6   8   9   7   5   3

LIBRARY
ALLEGANY COMMUNITY COLLEGE
Cumberland, Maryland

To

THE SMITHSONIAN INSTITUTION

keeper and catalyst of the exploring spirit

"An age will come after many years when the Ocean will loose the chain of things, and a huge land lie revealed; when Tiphys will disclose new worlds and Thule no more be the Ultimate."

—from Seneca's *Medea,* quoted by
Christopher Columbus' son,
Hernando, in a comment on his
father

CONTENTS

/ xi

☆   ☆   ☆

THE EXPLORING SPIRIT

AMERICA AND THE WORLD, THEN AND NOW

I

☆ THE BIRTH
☆ OF EXPLORATION ☆

When Columbus started out on his famous voyage, we are told, he didn't know where he was going, when he reached his destination he didn't know where he was, and when he got back he didn't know where he had been. Perhaps this quip has been popular because of a widespread suspicion, outside the United States, that it may describe us Americans during the whole two centuries of our national existence. But, like many other Old World characterizations of the relation between the Old World and the New, this gives the Old World hero too much credit.

For this suggests that Columbus really was an *explorer.* Actually, he was only a *discoverer,* although a very great one. The American experience stirred mankind from *discovery* to *exploration.* From the cautious quest for what they knew (or thought they knew) was out there, into an enthusiastic reaching to the unknown. These are two substantially different kinds of human enterprise.

FROM DISCOVERING TO EXPLORING

When we say that men climb the highest mountain "simply because it's there," we think we are describing changeless human nature. In fact, we are expressing a peculiarly modern point of view. Mountain-climbing is emphatically a modern sport. For most of human history, men not only feared the unknown, they shunned it. For millennia, people stood in awe of mountain peaks, glaciers, and all remote fastnesses. The English Historiographer Royal in the seventeenth century described the Alps as "high and hideous"—"uncouth huge monstrous excrescences of nature." A characteristic piece of mountain literature in the early eighteenth century was J. J. Scheuchzer's *Treatise on Alpine Dragons,* which discussed such interesting questions as whether the wingless dragons found in mountains were females of a species or were a species all their own. The prevailing view of the unexplored mountain landscape was expressed by Shelley:

> *This wall of eagle-baffling mountain,*
> *Black, wintry, dead, unmeasured; without herb,*
> *Insect, or beast, or shape or sound of life.*

The unknown and the forbidden were thought to be the same.

Not until the late eighteenth century did Europeans begin

to make a popular adventure of the effort to scale their mountains. The first recorded ascent of Mont Blanc, the highest mountain in Western Europe, was not until 1786. Climbing the mountain simply because it is there, is *not* an idea as old as the hills.

Mankind was slow to reach into the unknown. The unknown—"the undiscover'd country from whose bourn no traveller returns"—was the realm of death and devils. Sensible men would plot their adventures on maps of the familiar.

A glance at the best world maps of the late Middle Ages will instantly show us the meaning that America was destined to have for man's attitude toward his own knowledge. The great map of Fra Mauro (1459), now in the Biblioteca Marciana in Venice, commonly regarded as the climax of pre-Columbian cartography, shows the earth substantially covered by the continents, with only a thin fringe of water. The three "known" continents—Africa, Asia, Europe—are closely connected into "the island of the earth." Fra Mauro's map documented the dogma of the Book of Esdras (II, 6) in the Apocrypha, according to which the planet was covered six-sevenths by land and only one-seventh by water. In order to cover the sphere of the planet with so much land, it was necessary to extend Asia beyond its actual bounds and, at the same time, to reduce the oceans—all of which made the water distance from the Iberian peninsula westward to Asia seem conveniently short. It was such orthodox miscalculations as these that encouraged Columbus.

Fra Mauro's map, like other *mappae mundi,* was meant to be complete, a kind of wall atlas. Every city of considerable size was noted on it, with a tiny bird's-eye view of the characteristic architecture, and the appropriate animals round about on the landscape. On Fra Mauro's map there were no *terrae incognitae.* Any supposed "fourth part of the world" had no right to exist. There was no place to put it! All this helps us understand why Columbus was a discoverer and not an explorer. The crucial distinction between these two roles we can see in the origins of our English words. The etymology of the word "discover" is obvious. Its primary meaning is to uncover, or to disclose to view. The discoverer, then, is a *finder.* He shows us what he already knew was there. Columbus set out to "discover," to find, the westward oceanic route to Asia. Of course he knew the ocean, and he knew of Asia. He set out to find the way. The word "explore" has quite different connotations. Appropriately, too, it has a disputed etymology. Some say it comes from *ex* (out) and *plorare* (to cry out), on the analogy of "deplore." The better view appears to be that it comes from *ex* (out) and *plorare* (from *pluere,* to flow). Either etymology reminds us that the explorer is one who surprises (and so makes people cry out) or one who makes new knowledge flow out.

The discoverer simply uncovers, but the explorer opens. The discoverer concludes a search; he is a finder. The explorer begins a search; he is a seeker. And he opens the way for other seekers. The discoverer is the expert at what is known to be there. The explorer is willing to take chances. He is the adventurer who risks *un*certain paths to the *un*known. Every age is inclined to give its laurels to the discoverers, those who finally arrive at the long-thought-inaccessible known destination. But posterity—the whole human community—owes its laurels to the happener-upon dark continents of the earth and of the mind. The courageous wanderer in worlds never known to be there is the explorer.

It is plain that Columbus had the skills and the cast of mind of a discoverer. By the standards of his day, he was (as Samuel Eliot Morison has shown) a navigator of high expertise and wide experience. He was an able organizer, an effective commander. He thought he knew where he was going, he was convinced that he knew what he was looking for, and he believed—even insisted—that he had found what he went to discover. Columbus required members of his crew, under penalties, to swear that the land they reached was no mere island, but the "mainland" of Asia. According to his best biographers, he went to his death unaware (and unwilling to imagine) that the transatlantic lands he had touched were a New World. A great discoverer—we might even say an *obstinate* discoverer—but hardly a prophet of the exploring spirit.

Until someone seriously entertained the possibility of a new figment—a "fourth part of the world" in addition to Asia, Africa, and Europe—Europeans would continue to waste their ingenuity trying to make the Americas fit onto their crude cartography of Asia. Few other subjects have recently excited such scholarly passions as this question of who really "invented" America. The notorious *odium theologicum* has been matched by this *odium geographicum*. It was troublesome enough to have to revise Fra Mauro's map to find a place for whole new continents. But if the best maps of the world actually had left out so many lands, what did this mean for all the rest of knowledge? Perhaps it was not merely the maps of the planet that needed revising, but the whole map of knowledge.

The maps of the new age of exploration would bear a new

legend: "All the world which has been discovered *up to this time.*" "Up to this time!" These few words at the head of Diogo Ribeiro's world chart of 1529, a classic of the new geography, proclaimed the exploring spirit, the spirit of voyagers into the unknown, in search of they knew not what. This was the telltale clue that the imagination of Europe was about to be Americanized. Less by the land and treasure of the Western Hemisphere than by the simple discovery of the unknown. More's *Utopia* (1516), published only twenty-five years after Columbus' first voyage, was the imaginary report of a young man who had traveled to the New World with Amerigo Vespucci. As Edmund Spenser in *The Faerie Queene* (1589) observed:

> *But let that man with better sence advize,*
> *That of the world least part to us is red:*
> *And dayly how through hardy enterprize,*
> *Many great Regions are discovered,*
> *Which to late age were never mentioned.*
> *Who ever heard of th'Indian Peru?*
> *Or who in venturous vessell measured*
> *The Amazons huge river now found trew?*
> *Or fruitfullest Virginia who did ever vew?*
> *Yet all these were, when no man did them know;*
> *Yet have from wisest ages hidden beene:*
> *And later times things more unknowne shall show.*
> *Why then should witlesse man so much misweene*
> *That nothing is, but that which he hath seene?*

THE AMERICAN VOID

When British colonists settled in North America in the early seventeenth century, there were probably not more than three million Indians scattered over an area twice the size of Europe—which then had a population estimated at about one hundred million. Across the three-thousand-mile-wide continent, this indigenous population was spread thinly and sporadically. Within the area of the British seaboard colonies, American Indians had not developed an urban culture nor had they created large settled communities with which the English latecomers had to compete. The whole present area of the United States, compared to any other place where considerable numbers of Britons had settled, was a Void. "We can no longer say there is nothing new under the sun," Thomas Jefferson wrote to Joseph Priestley in 1801. "For this whole chapter in the history of man is new. The great extent of our republic is new. Its sparse habitation is new."

By contrast with North America, the other places to which European seafarers went at the beginning of the Age of the Sea (and the places toward which Columbus himself was aiming) were settled, even congested, communities. Vasco da Gama's first voyage to India was carefully planned to reach the very place where he arrived. He hoped to secure the well-known prized products available there. Laden with trade goods—striped cloth, scarlet hoods, hats, strings of coral, hand washbowls, sugar, oil, and honey—he finally reached his destination, Calicut, on the southwestern coast of the Indian peninsula. There he offered this merchandise to the Zamorin, the Hindu ruler of the place, who at first laughed, and then was insulted by such shoddy stuff. One of the most important pieces of information that da Gama brought back to Portugal was that future voyager-traders had better bring a quite different stock, preferably gold.

The piously repeated missionary purpose of the Portuguese—to convert the Muslim—would make sense only in populated places. This motive, too, led them to distant metropolises, with stops at cities on the way.

From this perspective, the Portuguese could hardly have seen the American Void as a desirable destination. Strange, then, that the vacancy of North America should prove to be its peculiar promise to the world. But emptiness was America's special fertility. This made it possible—and even necessary—for English settlers to organize their own communities, to transplant their institutions, and so start life afresh.

The great innovation in English philosophy in that first age of American settlement was John Locke's appeal to experience. His interesting suggestion could be summed up in the notion that at birth every man's mind was an America. The human mind, he said, was a *tabula rasa*—a blank sheet—on which the facts of life could inscribe their record, so making experience into knowledge. "In the Beginning," he observed, "all the world was America." He seized the American opportunity himself when he wrote his own constitution for the newly settled Carolinas.

By accident, the British came first upon an area where the native settlements were even sparser, less developed, and more shallow-rooted than those of some other parts of North America. But the Spanish first dominated areas to the west and south where the indigenous people had a more highly developed, focused, urban culture. Spanish missionary priests used the institutions that they found ready-made as their framework of control. The first great Spanish exploit in the Americas was Cortés' conquest of Mexico (1519), his notorious subjugation and betrayal of Montezuma to secure his treasure—a feat that was rivaled only thirteen years later by Pizarro's hijacking of the Emperor of the Incas of Peru. The Spanish, by the luck of the draw, which they had the courage and the ruthlessness to make the most of, became *conquistadores*. The English became colonists and settlers. The Spanish conquered the Aztecs and the Incas, the English conquered the land.

A contempt for the Indians would continue to mar the history of British settlements in North America. And it survived the centuries. While the Spanish and the Portuguese generally viewed the American Indians as peoples to be conquered, converted and assimilated, the English and their heirs commonly viewed the Indians as another hostile fixture of a wild landscape. Like the forests, they had to be cleared away.

EXPLORING IN COMMUNITY

The age that came upon a surprising "fourth part of the world" also saw what J. H. Parry has called "the Discovery of the Sea." And the era of Columbus witnessed "the victory of the caravel over the camel." The unpredicted revelation of so much more land on this planet was paralleled by an equally fertile revelation that the oceans were much vaster than had been imagined. In fact, to everybody's amazement, most of the planet was covered by a single planetary Ocean

Sea, and the oceans were interconnected, so that a good seaman with a proper ship could sail from any shore of any ocean to any other.

The modern maps would be charts of ocean highways, of the watery paths from anyplace to anyplace else. Medieval maps based on Ptolemy, whose Africa curved eastward, merging into China, had shown the Indian Ocean as a vast lake, a kind of Asiatic Mediterranean. If these maps had been correct, it would have been impossible to reach India by sailing around Africa. But even before Columbus, the oceans had begun to merge and open up. Fra Mauro's map modified Ptolemy to show the Indian Ocean as an open sea flowing round the tip of Africa.

As the voyages of Columbus and his followers enlarged men's vision of the land, so other voyages enlarged their vision of the sea. Magellan's "Discovery of the Sea," besides revealing that the earth was larger than had been imagined, also discovered a third ocean. This was, of course, what we now call the Pacific—stretching between Asia and America and bigger than either of the others.

When Magellan and his crew left the Atlantic and entered the Pacific going westward round Cape Horn at the tip of South America, they expected that the Pacific—then known to them only as the Great Gulf—could be crossed in a few weeks. They were taught their error in the most painful and persuasive way. At sea for nearly four months before they reached Guam, they kept alive by eating rats, chewing sawdust, gnawing leather, and scraping the barrels for powdered wormy biscuits. The Pacific Ocean, to their astonishment, covered one-third the area of the globe, and was equal to all the land masses of the world combined.

Still, the most important—if least celebrated—of the geographic discoveries of that age was that the oceans of the world were all connected. This meant, inevitably, that henceforth vast areas of European *mappae mundi* now would have to be left blank. *Terrae incognitae*—and *maria incognita*—which before had not even existed, now became enormous.

The British settlements in North America, as it happened, were the converging product of the revelation of twin unknowns: unknown continents and an unknown ocean. The Europeans who went to settle in America naturally profited from the new techniques of the Age of the Sea. "There is no sea innavigable," boasted Robert Thorne in 1527, "no land uninhabitable." The whole human destiny was being newshaped by the great seagoing vessels. Ships were bigger and better. Mariners now used new instruments—the quadrant, the sea-astrolabe and the cross-staff—to get their bearings by sun and stars, and could carry hundreds of passengers thousands of miles out of sight of land.

While the earlier traders to known places had carried merchants, sailors and soldiers, along with trading goods and a few missionary-priests, the first ships to the new "Plantations" in the American Void actually carried *communities*. Whole communities! Now, for the first time, whole communities could go as explorers—seeking into the unknown. While da Gama's fleet, the *São Gabriel*, the *São Rafael*, the *Berrio*, and their accompanying store-ship carried merchandise as their main cargo, the *Mayflower* carried people, together with all their tools for living. Among the *Mayflower*'s incidental undeclared cargo were such items as the Magna Charta, the Bible, and the unwritten traditions of the English constitution.

But the exploring communities did not end at the Atlantic seaboard. The whole remainder of the North American continent—much of it even into the nineteenth century still a Void—was an arena for American communities on the move. For at least two centuries, such communities could keep moving into new unknowns, enjoying the promise and the risks of exploration.

A simple way of explaining what made this new kind of community adventure possible was that Englishmen now had the Power to Leap. The sea was their floating medium, and the sizable vessels of the seventeenth and eighteenth centuries were their flying machines. Crossing the sea had become a vastly different experience from crossing the land.

Until the sixteenth century, the *land* was the common path that men followed even to the greatest distances. European travelers to the East in Marco Polo's day and the generation following usually went most of the way by land. Outside the Mediterranean, the main paths of long-distance trade, like the Silk Route across Western Asia into China, went overland. Land travel, too, tended to limit what could be carried to articles that were not bulky and yet were of high intrinsic value—in other words, luxury goods.

Now the sea opened all sorts of new possibilities, not only of what could be carried, but of who could go, and how far, and in what numbers. This new Power to Leap on the sea was not as melodramatic as the power to fly through the air which would come half a millennium later. But it was, in its own way, a power of flight—a power to go straight to raw and strange and distant places without passing through others in between.

The sea was wonderfully empty. That cultural emptiness

(like the American Void) would help explain much that would be possible in America. The enormous unpeopled Ocean Vacuum would become a precondition for revealing new possibilities in English institutions, for allowing whole communities to become explorers of an American unknown. Obviously, the colonists who came on shipboard at Plymouth in England would arrive at Plymouth in New England in the same cultural condition in which they had left. A prolonged community life on shipboard might bring them closer together, but gave no opening for extraneous cultural forces. Since there were no strange peoples, institutions, cultures, landscapes, or merchandise on the way, their six weeks' voyage of three thousand miles left them uncontaminated.

A trek of comparable length across any *land*scape would have been incomparably more enriching or contaminating. The English Crusaders who finally reached the Holy Land —after encounters with new products, new ideas, new languages, new religions—returned as quite different persons from those who had left. Such travels of Englishmen on land were important for the ideas or objects or ways of doing things that were picked up, lost, or exchanged on the way there and back. The newly charted Atlantic Ocean provided a medium through which English traditions, culture, and institutions could be carried securely ship-packaged—hermetically sealed for weeks—to be opened and tested at a strange destination.

The English settlements in America were not only outposts of empire, they were outposts of history. There the communities of Europeans who had leaped the ocean also leaped the centuries. In those whom they called "Indians" they saw how their primitive ancestors had lived in the primeval millennia. The "colonist" (the word had only lately come into the language in this sense) discovered that the centuries of progress had actually obscured many features of mankind, many possibilities of human community. He gradually awakened to unsuspected talents in himself and in his neighbors. He awakened to new ways for people to cluster together, new institutions to help men lean on one another. The opportunity which Sir Arthur Conan Doyle conceived in his *Lost World* had become an everyday experience for Americans—with the roles of dinosaur and brontosaurus having been played by rattlesnake and raccoon, bison and wapiti.

Modern European civilization, possessed of the achievements of Christendom, the liberalizing influence of Protestantism, the innovating spirit of the Renaissance, and the exploring vision of modern science, found itself in America suddenly on a scene of prehistory. When before had there been so intimate, so extensive, so vivid a confrontation of two such disparate stages in human development? When before had there been such communities of explorers, men joined together to discover new possibilities in the unknown?

This encounter between disparate epochs and disparate civilizations was an example of a Fertile Verge. For a *verge,* in my vocabulary of world history, is a boundary between anything and anything else—including, of course, the boundary between the known and the unknown, the familiar and the strange. This is a place where new ideas and new institutions grow, where new opportunities appear, where commerce in products and in thought can flourish. A verge is a kind of landscape—of the earth or of the mind—that makes

II

☆ FROM PILGRIM
FATHERS TO ☆
FOUNDING FATHERS

The great awakening of modern man was his finding out that life was not really as repetitious as it had always seemed. This proved to be one of the most difficult steps in human development. It was not easy to grasp the fact that experience was not merely a series of similar events, but an unfolding scene of exploration. America was to play a crucial role in this awakening.

Archaic man lived in the Age of Again-and-Again. "The thing that hath been," says the Book of Ecclesiastes, "it is that which shall be; and that which is done is that which shall be done: and there is no new thing under the sun." When men subsisted by their crops and their flocks, the return of the familiar was another name for security. The daily rising of the sun and the seasonal falling of the rain ensured grain for bread, and wool and skins for clothing. The good and the familiar seemed one. The unfamiliar, the strange, the out of the ordinary, was thought to be a miracle or a catastrophe.

In the world of biology, it was not until the late nineteenth century that learned men of Western Europe began to believe that novelty was really possible. More radical than the idea of the survival of the fittest was the notion that new species might emerge as time passed, that the existing world of plants and animals could be and was constantly being enriched. Until then, biology had described a world of rebirths. Each species created by God in the beginning was fruitful and multiplied "after his kind." But the idea of evolution changed biology into a world of revolutions. Older species were constantly being crowded out and extinguished. Nature was always in process of being dominated by the emerging new.

In the world of *human* community, the idea that novelty was possible and might be good had appeared even before Darwin. But its popularization, its laboratory demonstration, waited upon the American experience. How did America, and especially the United States, help mankind grasp this dangerous idea?

FROM RITUAL TO HISTORY

There is a hidden precision in the reverent cliché which describes the earliest New England settlers as Pilgrims. For a pilgrim is a religious devotee who journeys to a shrine or a sacred place. Pilgrimage—the characteristic popular travel-institution of the Age of Again-and-Again—is, of course, one of mankind's most ancient and most familiar rituals. In the late fourteenth century, Chaucer drew his wide social panorama describing the Canterbury pilgrims. These included all sorts and conditions of men and women—a miller, a knight, a nun, a sailor, a lawyer, a doctor, a merchant, a country gentleman, a cook, a carpenter, a haberdasher, and a miscellaneous dozen others. When such pilgrims traveled to a sacred place, they walked in the well-worn paths of the generations. The pilgrim went to reinforce his faith. Even though the trip to Mecca, to Benares, to Compostella, or to Canterbury often brought adventure, it was primarily not an exploration but a ritual.

When the first Puritans and Separatists came to New England, they too saw themselves going on a pilgrimage. Although the landscape would be unfamiliar, their mission would be familiar enough. New England would be their Zion. Their "City upon a Hill" would *re*build Jerusalem. The emptiness of America made it all the better for their pilgrimage. For when they had tried to rebuild Zion in the Netherlands, as Governor William Bradford of Plymouth Colony in New England reported, they found their children corrupted by "the great licentiousness of youth in that countrie, and the manifold temptations of the place . . . drawne away by evil examples into extravagante and dangerous courses, getting the raines off their neks, and departing from their parents."

In the American emptiness, they hoped, there could be no contagion from neighboring prodigals or heretics. Here the Pilgrim Fathers could keep their people pure. "Proclaime to the world, in the name of our Colony, that all Familists, Antinomians, Anabaptists, and other Enthusiasts, shall have free Liberty to keep away from us, and such as will come to be gone as fast as they can, the sooner the better."

The Pilgrim Fathers, then, did not see the New World as an opportunity to new-fashion society. Rather to old-fashion it to the perfect Biblical model. Wary of all newfangledness, they aimed not to "make history," but to fulfill theology. They hoped to repeat, more literally and more faithfully than anyone had ever done before, the ritual rebuilding of Zion. For them, city-building was not an enterprise in social science, but a religious rite.

Puritan theology had actually made social novelties impossible. God in the beginning had issued His catalogue of all life's possibilities. For the Bible was a catalogue of "types" (the modern sociologist would call them "models"). All later experience consisted only of the latter-day counterparts of those "types," which the Puritans called "antitypes." The plots of all possible human dramas had thus been revealed by God in the beginning. According to the Puritans' Biblical theology of Again-and-Again, men could play no roles except those which the Lord had long ago written in. When Samuel Sewall's infant son hid shamefacedly for some naughtiness he had committed, this was an antitype to Adam hiding himself after he had committed the original sin. Since their Puritan City upon a Hill was to be an antitype of ancient Jerusalem, the Bible was the only necessary textbook —of religion and ethics, of sociology, anthropology, and political science.

The shapers of American civilization and the makers of America's influence on the World Experience would not long continue to view their American mission in this way. New World experience and New World opportunities would effect a modern transformation. This was the transformation of a world of typology into a world of history. The archaic universe in which nothing could happen for the first time became one where unique events, new institutions, and unheard-of experiences were constantly emerging. In the unwittingly precise parlance of American patriotic clichés, this was the advance from a world of Pilgrim Fathers to a world of Founding Fathers. From Old World pilgrimage to New World enterprise.

In the earlier age to which the Pilgrim Fathers were heirs, the word "revolution" itself still had its original literal meaning. "Revolution" still meant a revolving—a turning cycle, a return of the familiar. Astronomers talked about the "revolutions of the spheres." Only later did "Revolution" begin to have its common modern meaning which emphasized not a cyclical return of the familiar, but a sudden turning to the new. The first recorded use of "Revolution" for an event in English history was in that now obsolete sense. It referred to the overthrow of the Rump Parliament in 1660, which resulted in the restoration of the monarchy. Then, after 1688, "revolution" was used to describe the expulsion of the Stuart dynasty of James II, and the transfer of sovereignty to William and Mary.

Yet this was only a mild and tentative approach to the new usage. The events of 1688 and 1689 which, with conspicuously un-English overstatement, came to be called "the Glorious Revolution," had occurred within the constitutional framework. Those events changed the powers of existing constitutional bodies, but did not bring into being new political entities.

"The American Revolution," by contrast, was cataclysmic. Two years before the Constitutional Convention in Philadelphia in 1787, David Ramsay had published his *History of the Revolution in South Carolina.* By 1789, Americans generally were referring to the recent war for Independence as a "Revolution."

Before that Revolution, in the very age when Americans were demonstrating the possibility of new beginnings, the English language was already faithfully recording the novelties entering the experience of all Western Europe. The word "explore," which had first appeared in its general meaning of "investigate" in the seventeenth century, came to mean "to search into or examine a country by going through it, to go into or range over for the purpose of discovery." About the same time, we find that the word "colony" which originally (from the Latin *colōnia*—drawn from *colonus,* meaning a farmer) had simply meant a farm or an estate in the countryside, was coming to denote a settlement in a new country. This use of the word provided Samuel Purchas with his delightful pun about Columbus (in Spanish, Cristóbal Colón), the discoverer of America: "O name Colón . . . which to the worlds end hast conducted Colonies." Appropriate new meanings of "colonize" and "colonist" soon followed. It was not until mid-eighteenth century that the English language brought into common use other words needed to chronicle the American experience: "emigrant" and "emigration." Their companion, "immigrant," came soon after. Within the next centuries, American experience would flood the language with new words, and would fill old words with new meanings.

America would be a place where the change in man's

attitude to his past was dramatized for all to see. The stage: the "fourth part of the world" which, until the early sixteenth century, Europeans had not even imagined to exist. The actors: the millions of people using unprecedented resources of the Age of the Sea, the Age of Ocean-Faring, to transplant themselves across thousands of miles. The theme: the building of new communities on a rich continental emptiness.

Was there anywhere on earth any conceivable set of circumstances (short of voyages to outer space) better suited to revise and enlarge man's view of all human experience? Not to relive Biblical "types," but to create unique modern forms? Any experience better designed than the American to persuade man that his destiny on this planet was not ritual, but history?

Needless to say, the instruments for modern man's escape from the archaic world of Again-and-Again were not invented in America. The Renaissance (as historians Peter Burke and Ricardo J. Quinones have lately shown) brought Europe to a revised sense of time. The past would no longer be a landscape of repeated undulations and relived cycles, but would be revealed as ever-changing. The lessons would be overshadowed by the pageant. The human chronicle would not be a catalogue of the familiar, but a kaleidoscope of unpredictables.

This simple notion that experience was full of the unique and the unprecedented would be one of the most drastic of modern inventions. History (in both senses of the word) had to be invented. A galaxy of European artists, poets, and thinkers from Petrarch, Vasari, and Shakespeare to Harrington, Clarendon, and Locke prepared people for the shock. America, notably the United States of America, was a proving ground for this world-shaking idea.

VISIBLE BEGINNINGS

Before the founding of the United States, cities and nations had been born in the mists of mythology. Romulus and Remus, twin sons of the vestal virgin Rhea Silvia and the god Mars, were suckled by a she-wolf until they were adopted by a shepherd. After Romulus was chosen by an omen to found the new city (753 B.C.), he brought fugitives there as the first settlers and secured wives for them by leading the Rape of the Sabine Women. Finally, after a long reign, he disappeared in a thunderstorm, to be worshiped ever after as the god Quirinus. King Arthur, a mighty Welsh warrior first mentioned in epics of the seventh century, fought a dozen battles against Saxon invaders, and by the twelfth century was reputed to have been the conqueror of Western Europe, even before he became the central figure in the legendary quest for the Holy Grail.

In those days, whatever was lacking in facts was wonderfully repaired by imagination—then reported and immortalized by epic poets. The chronicle of Rome's new beginnings became Virgil's *Aeneid,* and Britain's Arthurian legend was repeatedly enriched for over a thousand years—from the Welsh poem *Gododdin* and Geoffrey of Monmouth to Sir Thomas Malory and Lord Tennyson.

To all this mythic wealth the United States, which reached its two hundredth birthday in 1976, has offered a striking contrast. Our nation was founded in the bright light of history. During the whole nineteenth century, what was considered most remarkable about the birth of the United States was that it was so recent. Even from the late twentieth-century perspective, we can describe the United States, in Seymour Martin Lipset's phrase, as "the First New Nation." In our time, when the conceiving of new nations (for which there is no contraceptive) overpopulates the councils of the United Nations, we are apt to forget how novel the new United States must have seemed back in the late eighteenth century.

The United States was not merely the first New Nation. It would also be the first prosaic nation, the first nation which, strictly speaking, was both conceived and born within history. By contrast with the mysterious poetic gestation, the divinely performed Caesarean births of others, the United States was a plainly human product. There were already plenty of examples in recent times of the death or suppression of ancient "nations." In the British Isles alone there were the three examples of Scotland, Wales, and Ireland. But the *birth*—or perhaps more properly, the fabrication—of a nation—that was another story. It was a stunning novelty.

The idea that a new nation could be made at all sent out shock waves that reached over the world and into later centuries. Its impact was both negative and positive. On the negative side, the founding of the United States revealed that a functioning nation (normal in all other respects) did *not* need an ancient pedigree nor require the midwifery of a Mars, a Siegfried, or a King Arthur. On the positive side, the founding of the United States revealed that nations could be brought into being expressly to serve the convenience, the needs, and the ambitions of living men and women. The living were no longer at the mercy of the dead. By forethought, collaboration, courage, and hard work, they could create a nation for themselves and their contemporaries, and for their posterity.

The essentially new American idea for political theorists was not the idea of representative government. Britain, not America, was the Mother of Parliaments, and republican institutions had deep roots elsewhere in Europe. In the English language, a century before the American Revolution, there was already an extensive, profound, and respectable literature of self-government. The Americans plainly and repeatedly declared their loyalty to this republican tradition. The Constitution of the United States of America, unlike basic legal documents before it, was announced not in the name of any divinity or any divinely appointed King, but in the name of "We, the People."

Another American novelty—in a world not yet quite accustomed to novelty in political institutions—came along quite naturally with the belief that a living generation could create a new nation. This was the special meaning which the Americans would attach to "the People." To this peculiar overtone Thomas Jefferson gave eloquent and prophetic expression. "We may consider each generation as a distinct nation," he observed, "with a right, by the will of its majority, to bind themselves, but none to bind the succeeding generation, more than the inhabitants of another country." And Jefferson spelled out the consequences:

No society can make a perpetual constitution, or even a perpetual law. The earth belongs always to the living generation: they may manage it, then, and what proceeds from it, as they please. . . . They are masters, too, of their own persons, and consequently may govern them as they please. . . . The constitution and the laws of their predecessors are extinguished then, in their natural course, with those whose will gave them being. . . . If it be enforced longer, it is an act of force, and not of right.

Of course, political thinkers and revolutionaries had repeatedly asserted the right of the living to liberate themselves from inherited abuses. Here was something else—not merely an outcry against the tyranny of the past, but a declaration of the Sovereignty of the Present.

More than that, here would be a living example of how a new nation could be built by the present generation. Paradoxically, the Founding Fathers' hopes that this nation would last far into the future rested on their faith in the fluidity of its foundations—in its capacity to be reshaped continually to the changing will of each future generation. The United States, then, rested on the shockingly simple notion that nation-building was not the monopoly of gods and ancestors, that it could be a do-it-yourself activity.

To secularize and de-mystify the origins of nations would have a profound effect on the world. American thinking, too, not only about politics but about nearly everything else, was overcast by this reality: the Visible Beginnings of countless institutions, technologies, ways of life, and communities of transplanted peoples.

The making of the United States was both historic and historical. America was to be the land not merely of the new, but of the recorded, visible new. Was man's power to innovate somehow rooted in his ability and his desire to keep an accurate record of his experience? People here would be newly aware of what they were doing that had not been done before. Man's capacity to bring novelty into his experience thus grew right along with his capacity to see and to record what he was doing. The making of the United States witnessed a signal expansion of human self-consciousness.

A symbol of this was James Madison, who is often called "the Father of the Constitution." For Madison was both the principal architect of the Constitution and the principal recorder of the acts of its creation. Madison's eyewitness record of the Constitutional Convention was the first such laboratory notebook of an experiment in nation-making. To this day, his *Notes* remain the best single source for our knowledge of the historic events in Independence Hall in Philadelphia in 1787.

The special features of the American Visible Beginning have become so familiar that it is hard for us to realize their innovative power at the time of the birth of the United States.

Controversy and Debate. The framework of this new nation (despite the enthusiastic hyperbole of superpatriots) was not given from on high. It emerged from the conversation and debates of men whose names and lives we know, and from their outspoken disagreement. The meetings in Philadelphia in the summer of 1787 were the product of earlier meetings, and were to provide the occasion for still other controversial meetings up and down the Atlantic seaboard. Those prudent and thoughtful men, not in the habit of wasting their breath, found it worthwhile to prepare lengthy speeches, to marshal facts and answer objections. Parliamentary debate was no novelty in 1787, and had reached a high art in England in the speeches of William Pitt, Edmund Burke, and others. But these Americans now were not simply choosing among alternative measures for an established government. They were debating the very shape of government, the essential character of their new nation.

Compromise as an Institution. Another vivid American proof that governments need not be the work of gods or mythical heroes, but could be the work of self-governing inventive people, was the prominence of compromise. The crucial events of the Convention were not classic statements of theory or of dogma, but a certain number of compromises. The Constitutional Convention in fact elevated compromise into an American institution, which would remain the main instrument of American political creativity. The struggles in the Convention were for the most part not clashes of ideologies, but conflicts of interests. The best textbook histories of American constitution-making rightly describe the compromises as the main themes of the Convention. Compromises embodied in a constitution—another name for the federal system—could make everything else possible.

Amendment as an Institution. The amending process was itself a compromise. And it was an embodied declaration of the Sovereignty of the Present (not just the present Present, but the future Present). The Founding Fathers (in another crucial compromise) devised machinery to enable each generation to be sovereign over its own constitution. That the so-called "Bill of Rights" was itself a kind of compromise was revealed when it appeared in the form of the first ten amendments. Since that time, several of the sixteen later amendments to the Constitution have had a character less than constitutional—for example, the so-called "Prohibition

Amendment," which aimed to outlaw the saloon and instead created the speakeasy and helped finance organized crime. But, by and large, the amendments that have been adopted have been basic. The Founding Fathers did not try to restrict the scope of Amendment—except to delay the possibility of certain amendments for twenty years (till 1808), and to forbid any change in the equal representation of the States in the Senate. But even this qualification was needed to preserve the Federal framework, which was the very machinery of compromises. Had the authors of the Constitution circumscribed the amending power of future generations, we later generations might have been left with no constitution to amend.

This Visible Beginning of the new nation dramatized as seldom before the power of a living generation over its institutions. The fluidity of the new government expressed the Founding Fathers' wholesome awareness of the limits of their power over the future. If they had lacked this vivid modern sense of either the extent or the limits of their power, it is doubtful that the Constitution which created the United States of America could have survived for two centuries, to outlive all other written constitutions. This is another way of saying that the Founding Fathers possessed a lively sense of history. The modern spirit was emphatically history-conscious. A changing present had liberated mankind from the world of Again-and-Again.

A CONTINENT-WIDE LABORATORY

The creating of this new nation by the Federal Constitution dramatized modern man's capacity to make history. Then the filling out of the continent by the self-conscious new-fashioning of States would show that institution-founding was not the monopoly of a Founding Generation. Across the continent, men whose talents were surely no match for those of Franklin and Madison and James Wilson would dare to new-fashion their own States. The United States of America grew and took shape from just such acts of creation. In each new State, from Ohio to California, and from Florida to Oregon, there was new proof that people could make their own institutions. Novelty became an American tradition.

In England, the origins of cities were shrouded in prehistoric mist. But as Americans spread west, they casually founded new cities with enthusiasm, optimism, and ingenuity. Even when they borrowed past glory by calling their settlements Cairo, Athens, Rome, or London, they affirmed that by transplanting metropolitan grandeur *they* could do what earlier generations had not done. English institutions of higher learning had foundations deep in ancient charters, reaching back to the Middle Ages. By the time of the American Revolution there were still only two degree-granting institutions in England, but there were already nine in the United States, where the energy of a living generation made medieval charters superfluous.

Not only constitution-making but law-making flourished in the United States. While England somehow has managed with a single Parliament, the United States eventually provided itself with fifty-one legislative bodies, each making laws to serve its current purposes. The idea of law-making itself, we too easily forget, was not ancient. In England, even into the seventeenth century, it was the "High *Court* of Parliament." Parliament had remained primarily a law-declaring, not a law-making body. Its duty was *jus dicere*, not *jus dare*. From that archaic world of Again-and-Again came the sanctity of the fundamental law, which was nothing more or less than custom "to which the mind of man runneth not to the contrary." The law was what you could prove had been done by the appropriate authority again and again. While England came only gradually to the possibilities of legislation, of new-fashioning laws to serve present needs, the American nation was actually born in that discovery. And the United States would become perhaps the most legislated nation on earth.

III

☆ THE THERAPY ☆
OF DISTANCE

With the settlement of the colonies in North America, for the first time in history the English "provinces" became transatlantic. The story of American civilization gives us an opportunity to see what happens when a prospering old culture detaches a piece of itself to a great distance. On the other side of a broad ocean, the civilization of Englishmen became something it never could have become within their little island. "Not a place upon earth might be so happy as America," Thomas Paine observed in 1776. "Her situation is remote from all the wrangling world, and she has nothing to do but to trade with them." But that was not the whole story.

SELF-GOVERNMENT FROM NECESSITY

The American colonies were not, of course, the first settlements of Englishmen outside of England. There was an ancient distinction in constitutional law, as Charles H. McIlwain has shown, between the *realm* of England (England itself) and the *dominions* (other lands "belonging to" England). The American colonies were not the first testing ground of the capacity of the English Constitution to provide machinery for self-government beyond the island.

In the seventeenth century, while Englishmen in America were building colonies, the Irish, separated by only a few miles of water, were trying without success to assert their right to legislate for themselves. The English Commonwealth Parliament of 1649, with the arrogance of a parvenu, declared that the English Parliament alone ("the People . . . without any King or House of Lords") should have the power to govern England and "all the Dominions and Territories thereunto belonging." The very same Declaration which proclaimed England "to be a Commonwealth and Free-State" thus silently declared that Ireland had no right to govern itself. Free Englishmen asserted their right to make laws for all those whom they "possessed." For the first time there emerged into constitutional parlance the notion of "British Possessions." The irony of this situation, which escaped most English statesmen, was vivid enough to the dyspeptic Irishman Jonathan Swift, who called "government without the consent of the governed . . . the very definition of slavery." The Irish, Swift noted, were well enough equipped with arguments, "but the love and torrent of power prevailed. . . . in fact, eleven men well armed will certainly subdue one single man in his shirt."

Ireland was too close to England, and the stakes of the Irish Empire too great, for the Irish prophets of Revolution to prevail. The Irish proponents of self-government lost. Before the settlement of the American colonies, the only place in the English dominions (i.e., outside England) where the right to self-government was successfully asserted was in the tiny Channel Islands, which neither threatened nor promised enough to justify a battle. The doughty Channel Islanders had the gall to argue that if *anyone* was dependent on anyone else, the English were dependent on *them,* since they were the remaining fragment of the Dukedom of Normandy, whose William had conquered England.

While Cromwell's Army could master next-door Ireland, neither he nor his successors could preserve the power of the English Parliament over these thirteen colonies of transatlantic Americans. Three thousand miles of ocean accomplished what could not be accomplished by a thousand years of history. The Atlantic Ocean proved a more effective advocate than all the constitutional lawyers of Ireland.

The significance of sheer distance appears from the earliest settlement of Englishmen in the New World. Here is how William Bradford describes what happened in mid-November, 1620, when he and the other Pilgrim Fathers had their first view of the American coast:

> . . . after longe beating at sea they fell with that land which is called Cape Cod; the which being made and certainly knowne to be it, they were not a litle joyfull. After some deliberation had amongst them selves and with the master of

the ship, they tacked aboute and resolved to stande for the southward (the wind and weather being faire) to finde some place aboute Hudsons river for their habitation. But after they had sailed that course aboute halfe the day, they fell amongst deangerous shoulds and roring breakers, and they were so farr intangled ther with as they conceived them selves in great danger; and the wind shrinking upon them withall, they resolved to beare up againe for the Cape, and thought them selves hapy to gett out of those dangers before night overtooke them, as by Gods providence they did. And the next day they gott into the Cape-harbor wher they ridd in saftie.

If the Pilgrim Fathers had been closer to home or more accurate in their navigation or luckier in their weather, it is most unlikely that there ever would have been any need for the "Mayflower Compact." That document, which Bradford called "the first foundation of their govermente in this place," was to be the primary document of self-government in the British colonies in North America.

The legal right of these English separatists to settle in the New World came from a patent which they had received from the Virginia Company of London, who authorized them to establish "a particular plantation" wherever they wished within the domain of the Company. The Pilgrims had intended to settle at the mouth of the Hudson River, which was still well within the Virginia Company's northern boundaries. If they had landed there, their patent from the Virginia Company would have sufficed, and they would have had no need for a fundamental instrument of government.

But Cape Cod, where the Pilgrims actually found themselves, was too far north and so outside the Virginia Company's domain. By settling at Plymouth they put themselves in a state of nature. Their patent was not valid there. They were now within the jurisdiction of the Northern Virginia Company (at that time being reorganized into the Council for New England), from whom they had no patent. They would have to create their own government. This they did with the Mayflower Compact, written on board their vessel and signed on November 11, 1620, by forty-one men, including every head of a family, every adult bachelor, and most of the menservants. The only males who did not affix their names were two sailors who had signed on the voyage for a single year, and the other passengers who happened to be under the legal age of discretion.

The accident of misnavigation, as Bradford reported, had been noticed by some of the more legalistic and libertarian *Mayflower* passengers and became an urgent reason for hastily creating some document of self-government. The Compact which they wrote so quickly was "occasioned partly by the discontented and mutinous speeches that some of the strangers amongst them had let fall from them in the ship; Thate when they came a shore they would use their owne libertie; for none had power to command them, the patente they had being for Virginia, and not for New-england, which belonged to an other Goverment, with which the Virginia Company had nothing to doe."

The government which the *Mayflower* colonists created by their Compact was, according to Bradford, "as firme as any patent, and in some respects more sure." They wrote a new chapter in the history of self-government. For in other places the roots of civil government had been buried deep under the debris of time. America laid bare the birth of government where it would be plain for all to see. In 1802 at Plymouth, in an often reprinted oration, John Quincy Adams extolled the Mayflower document as "perhaps the only instance, in human history, of that positive, original social compact, which speculative philosophers have imagined as the only legitimate source of government."

It was appropriate that the occasion for the primeval document of American self-government should have come not from ideology but from a simple fact of life. That was what New England historians have straightforwardly called "the missing of the place." In America, need and opportunity upstaged ideology.

In their American remoteness the New Englanders created simple new forms of self-government. The New England town meetings had an uncertain precedent in the vestry meetings of rural England, but American circumstances gave town meetings comprehensive powers and a new vitality. Once again, Americans relived the mythic prehistory of government. Tacitus had sketched that prehistory in his account of popular assemblies among the Germanic tribes. It also could be glimpsed in the direct democracy of the Swiss Landsgemeinde (the popular assembly of the self-governing canton) which flourished from the thirteenth till the seventeenth century. Even as the direct democracy of the Swiss cantons was declining, it was being reborn in New England.

From the beginning, New England facts transcended Old English forms. The New England town meetings, which met first weekly, then monthly, came to include all the men who had settled the town. At first, the meetings seem to have been confined to so-called "freemen," those who satisfied the legal requirements for voting in the colony. Soon the towns developed their own sort of "freemen"—a group larger than those whom the General Court of the colony recognized as grantees of the land. While the town meetings proved to be lively and sometimes acrimonious debating societies, they were more than that. They distributed town lands, they levied local taxes, they made crucial decisions on schools, roads, and bridges, and they elected the selectmen, constables, and others to conduct town affairs between the meetings.

The laws of Massachusetts Bay Colony gradually gave form to the town meetings. A law of 1692 required that meetings be held annually in March and enumerated the officers to be elected. A law of 1715 required the selection of moderators, gave them the power to impose fines on those who spoke without permission during meetings, and authorized any ten or more freeholders to put items on the agenda. But as the movement for Independence gathered momentum, Britain's Parliamentary Act of 1774 decreed that no town meeting should be held to discuss affairs of government without written permission from the royal Governor.

The transatlantic distance had given to these transplanted Englishmen their opportunity and their need to govern themselves. The tradition of self-government, which had been established in England by the weight of hundreds of years, was being established in America by the force of hundreds of miles.

What the Mayflower Compact and the town meetings did for the earliest New England settlers, the State constitutions and numerous State legislatures accomplished for later Americans spreading across the continent. The United States would have its Civil War, its war for secession. But, significantly, that war was fought between segments of the original seaboard colonies, and was involved with deep moral issues and the conflict of economic interests. Of the more remote States, only Utah—the Mormon community—would offer any substantial threat of secession.

In the growing United States, paradoxically, distance itself had nourished institutional safeguards against rebellion. Because the States grew in the American Void, as they grew they were free to develop and had to develop their own forms of self-government. The American Add-a-State plan was not confused by ancient imperial ties. The government of each new unit was shaped by and for the new settlers. The main sufferers from this system were the American Indians, who were already there and whom the new settlers treated as mere obstacles to be removed. The "mother country" headquartered in Washington speedily abandoned efforts to impose its will on remote parts. Paradoxically, the American federal system, and especially the equality of States in the United States Senate, made it possible for these western "colonies" gradually to dominate the politics of the Eastern Seaboard "mother country."

ANTIDOTES TO MONOPOLY

Just as the American remoteness dissolved the powers of the imperial bureaucrats in London over the lives of transplanted Englishmen, so too it dissolved numerous petty bureaucracies. Daily life in the English homeland was a domain of specialized monopolies. The nation labored under the burden of privileged guilds and chartered companies which had divided all the subjects' needs into profitable satrapies.

In seventeenth-century England, the command of armies had become an aristocratic monopoly. While the private soldiers tended to be the social dregs drawn from jails and taverns, the officers were usually aristocratic gentlemen who had bought or inherited their commands. This feature of European armies had certain wholesome and even pleasant consequences. It helped produce an Age of Limited Warfare that might equally have been called an Age of Ceremonial Warfare. Members of an international aristocracy were versed in the "rules" of war for civilized nations which were recorded in the writings of Grotius and Vattel. The conduct of battles was a real-life version of chess. "Now it is frequent," Daniel Defoe observed in 1697, "to have armies of fifty thousand men of a side stand at bay within view of one another, and spend a whole campaign in dodging, or, as it is genteelly called, observing one another, and then march off into winter quarters. The difference is in the maxims of war, which now differ as much from what they were formerly as long perukes do from piqued beards, or as the habits of the people do now from what they then were. The present maxims of war are—

> Never fight without a manifest advantage,
> And Always encamp so as not to be forced to it.

And if two opposite generals nicely observe both these rules, it is impossible they should ever come to fight." It is not surprising that between engagements the officers of opposing sides entertained one another with balls, concerts, and dinner parties.

In America, the profession of arms was being dissolved into communities of citizen-soldiers—not through force of dogma, but through force of circumstances. Firearms were a daily necessity—both for gathering food and skins, and for defense against the Indians. "A well grown boy at the age of twelve or thirteen years," a settler observed in the Valley of Virginia in the 1760's, "was furnished with a small rifle and shot-pouch. He then became a fort soldier, and had his port-hole assigned him. Hunting squirrels, turkeys and raccoons, soon made him expert in the use of his gun."

Of course, the American Indians had never read Grotius or Vattel and were ignorant of European military etiquette. They were skilled, courageous, and ruthless guerrilla fighters, and the colonists had to follow their example. Back-woods warfare was nothing like the polite game of military chess described by Defoe. It was individualistic warfare, warfare without rules, which dissolved all sorts of distinctions— between officer and private, and even between soldier and civilian.

The military profession was only one of the monopolies that dissolved in the American remoteness. "Besides the hopes of being safe from Persecution in this Retreat," William Byrd wrote in 1728, "the New Proprietors [of New Jersey] inveigled many over by this tempting account of the Country: that it was a Place free from those 3 great Scourges of Mankind, Priests, Lawyers, and Physicians. Nor did they tell a word of a Lye, for the People were as yet too poor to maintain these Learned Gentlemen." But as important as their poverty was the sheer distance of the colonists from the Old World citadels of privilege.

In religion, the remoteness of America and the vast spaces in America made it impossible to preserve the monopoly of the Established Church. The Puritans in New England were not noted for their toleration. They warned away all heretics and they harried the Quakers from their midst. Meanwhile, Rhode Island, Connecticut, and Pennsylvania gladly welcomed refugees. And the American backwoods proved to be a boundlessly tolerating landscape. There was room enough for everybody. "If New England be called a Receptacle of Dissenters, and an Amsterdam of Religion," the Reverend Hugh Jones of Virginia wrote in 1724, "Pennsylvania the Nursery of Quakers, Maryland the Retirement of Roman Catholicks, North Carolina the Delight of Buccaneers and Pyrates, Virginia may be justly esteemed the happy Retreat of true Britons and true Churchmen for the most part. . . ." But even in Virginia, as Jones observed, "the Parishes being of great Extent, Every Minister is a kind of Independent in his own Parish." Commonly, there was no nearby church where the prescribed ceremonies could be performed. "In Houses also there is Occasion, from Humour, Custom sometimes, from Necessity most frequently, to baptize Children and church Women, otherwise some would go without it. In Houses also they most commonly marry, without Regard to the Time of the Day or Season of the Year." The wonderful independence and variety of American religions never ceased to amaze the visitors from abroad. In 1828, Mrs. Trollope found the churchgoing Americans "insisting upon having each a little separate banner, embroidered with a device of their own imagining." She wrote, "The whole people appear to be divided into an almost endless variety of religious factions."

In England, the higher learning as well as religion had been a monopoly of the Established Church. Nonconformists had difficulty securing admission to Oxford or Cambridge (the only English universities till the early nineteenth century), while Catholics and Jews were absolutely excluded. The dissenting academies, which set high scholarly standards, had no power to grant degrees. In America, by contrast, at the time of the Revolution, nearly every major Christian sect had a degree-granting institution of its own. By the early eighteenth century, New England Puritans and their secessionists had set up Harvard and Yale, while Virginia conformists of the Church of England had their College of William and Mary. The flourishing variety of sects nourished a variety of institutions. New-Side Presbyterians founded Princeton University; revivalist Baptists founded Brown University in Rhode Island; Dutch Reformed revivalists founded Queen's College (later Rutgers University) in New Jersey; a Congregational minister transformed an Indian missionary school into Dartmouth College in New Hampshire; Anglicans and Presbyterians joined in founding King's College (later Columbia University) in New York City and the College of Philadelphia (later the University of Pennsylvania).

Americans were happily distant from the metropolitan headquarters in London of the monopolies of the medical and the legal professions. That was where professional guilds guarded their antique silver, displayed their charters, and organized to keep out competitors. And where they preserved pedantic distinctions among their several branches. The aristocrats of the legal profession were the "barristers" fortified in their London Inns of Court which held the power to admit to the bar, and the monopoly of practice before the High Courts. "Attorneys," while not authorized to plead in court, set the machinery of the court in motion. Then there were the "solicitors," private legal agents whose province it was to look after routine legal matters. Besides these there were "notaries" (organized in their Scriveners' Company) who prepared the documents that required a notarial seal, in addition to patent agents, and still other specialists. Their English citadel was London—but there was no American London.

In America, legal specialties dissolved and there were citizen-lawyers. When the young John Adams in 1758 sought the advice of a leading Boston lawyer on the requirements for the practice, he was advised that "a lawyer in this country must study common law, and civil law, and natural law, and admiralty law; and must do the duty of a counsellor [barrister], a lawyer, an attorney, a solicitor, and even of a scrivener." As the standard of technical competence was lower than in England, even the distinction between lawyer and layman was blurred. Of the nine Chief Justices of Massachusetts between 1692 and the Revolution, only three had specialized legal training. American businessmen were more inclined to be their own lawyers. Land, which in England was an heirloom and the most metaphysical of legal subjects, in America became a commodity. When landownership was widely diffused, its mysteries seemed less arcane.

Few expressed the American suspicion of professional monopolists better than Samuel Livermore, who was Chief

Justice of the New Hampshire Supreme Court in the late eighteenth century. He lacked legal learning himself, and as a contemporary reported he "did not like to be pestered with it in his courts." "When [counsel] attempted to read law books in a law argument, the Chief Justice asked him why he read them; 'if he thought that he and his brethren did not know as much as those musty old worm-eaten books?'" One of Livermore's brethren on the bench (himself a farmer and trader by occupation) charged a jury "to do justice between the parties not by any quirks of the law out of Coke or Blackstone—books that I never read and never will—but by common sense as between man and man."

We must keep all this in mind when we recall that of the fifty-six signers of the Declaration of Independence twenty-five were self-styled "lawyers," and of the fifty-five members of the Constitutional Convention in Philadelphia thirty-one were lawyers. These facts were not so much evidence of the peculiar importance of legal learning as they were symptoms of the decline of monopolies in America. "In no country perhaps in the world," Edmund Burke observed in his speech *On Conciliation with the American Colonies (1775),* "is the law so general a study . . . all who read, and most do read, endeavor to obtain some smattering in that science." The multiplying American legislatures, enough to provide a seat for nearly any citizen who was so inclined, helped bring into being the citizen-lawyer.

A similar American catharsis occurred in the medical professions. The eighteenth-century English patient suffered from the doctors' many sub-monopolies. At the top of the social scale, corresponding to the barrister, was the "Doctor of Physick," who enjoyed the privileges of the Royal College of Physicians chartered by Henry VIII back in 1518. But his professional ethics, rooted in the clerical tradition of the two English Universities, forbade him to shed blood or handle the human body. The "barber-surgeons," who had been organized in 1540, were later split by the distinction between the "barbers," who had a monopoly on cutting hair, shaving beards, and extracting teeth, and the "surgeons," who performed other operations. Besides these were the "apothecaries," who until 1617 had been the members of the grocers' guild, but thereafter had a monopoly on selling drugs. And in addition, there were the "midwives," who till the end of the seventeenth century were generally women and who had to be licensed by their bishop.

In colonial America, where distances were great and specialists scarce, all such monopolists gave way to the general practitioner. "I make use of the English word doctor," wrote the observant Marquis de Chastellux, who traveled the colonies in 1781, "because the distinction of physician is as little known in the army of Washington as in that of Agamemnon. We read in Homer, that the physician Macaon himself dressed the wounds. . . . The Americans conform to the ancient custom and it answers very well."

The therapy of distance worked in countless other ways. Distinctions of social classes, which in Europe had been reinforced by all these other distinctions, did not survive intact in the New World. Since the witty drawing rooms, learned libraries, genteel academies, and grand council-chambers of the Old World were an ocean away, Americans could not escape some provincial crudity and naïveté. But the ocean also separated them from the irrelevancies of a

LIBRARY
ALLEGANY COMMUNITY COLLEGE
Cumberland, Maryland

filigreed society, from Old World pomposity and pride and priggishness, from traditional conceits and familial arrogance. Americans would discover for themselves the wisdom in Jonathan Swift's ironic Irish view, "If a man makes me keep my distance, the comfort is, he keeps his at the same time." And American experience would show the world what a purging could do for ancient institutions.

IV

THE DARK CONTINENT
☆   OF TECHNOLOGY: ☆
THE POWER TO LEAP

The conduct of daily life for Americans in the later twentieth century would not follow the rules which had governed experience at the time of our nation's founding. Technology would tend to neutralize or destroy some peculiar American opportunities. For those had arisen out of the special situation of the North American continent in space, and the special situation of the birth of the United States in time. In our later age, the therapy of distance, the shock of visible beginnings, the very meaning and potency of history would be diluted or dissipated.

The meaning of physical distance was transformed. The new technology was the conscious product of imaginative and energetic individual men and women, and of potent new institutions. But its consequences extended beyond the ken of the inventors. These seeping, pervasive, interstitial, unexpected consequences would become the daily problems and opportunities of twentieth-century Americans and eventually might become those of all mankind.

THE DISTANT NO LONGER REMOTE

Back in 1748, the pioneer French sociologist Baron de Montesquieu, whose works were well known to the authors of the Declaration of Independence, had argued that a republic could endure only if confined to a small territory. Only then, he said, would the public interest be simple enough to be comprehended by the people. Many of the Founding Fathers of the American republic agreed. When Patrick Henry argued against ratifying the federal constitution in the Virginia Convention, on June 9, 1788, he challenged the Federalists to produce "a single example" of a great extent of country governed by one Congress. "One government," he insisted, "cannot reign over so extensive a country as this is, without absolute despotism." The War for American Independence had been fought against government-at-a-distance from abroad. Would government-at-a-distance on the American continent be any more tolerable?

Even those, like James Madison, who championed the new Constitution, noted dangers in the large reach of the new confederacy. But in *The Federalist* they argued that American geography could provide a built-in safeguard against the threat of centralized government. That safeguard was the variety of interests to be found in the wide extent of the American colonies. If a large nation would offer the danger of government-at-a-distance, it might also offer the salutary checks and balances of a heterogeneous continent. Thomas Jefferson made precisely this point after his party won the election of 1800. "Had our territory been even a third of what it is," he observed, "we were gone. But while frenzy and delusion like an epidemic, gained certain parts, the residue remained sound and untouched and held on till their brethren could recover from the temporary delusion; and that circumstance has given me great comfort."

The importance of sheer distance in shaping American political thought appeared again and again and in obvious ways. This federal republic assigned all the "police powers" —the lion's share of legislation and administration—to the political unit which was closer to the citizen. For a citizen's concern and his knowledge of affairs were supposed to be directly proportionate to his closeness to the problem. The Constitution therefore gave to the central government only certain specified powers, and left all the rest to the States. In foreign policy, too, the force of distance became an axiom that was soon translated into policy. In 1823, the Monroe Doctrine declared the American determination to preserve the oceans as a moat-protective, to enforce quarantine from the many ills "on that side of the Atlantic."

By the twentieth century, technology in the United States had done much to destroy the power of distance. Of course, the twin technologies of transportation and communication played the largest role. The most influential American successes in these areas have been (for transportation) the automobile and the airplane, and (for communication) the radio and television. Nothing was more obvious. But some of the indirect consequences of the American conquest of distance were less obvious. Perhaps the most important social by-product was a fantastic increase in man's Power to Leap.

To understand this we must recall how, five centuries earlier, seafaring Europeans had first acquired a Power to Leap. In the Age of the Sea the progress of technology and of geographic, astronomic, and scientific knowledge—man's newly amplified Power to Leap—had made possible the "discovery" and then the settlement of America. By the early sixteenth century Europeans had developed the means to carry communities through the cultural vacuum of thousands of ocean-miles, by-passing everything in between. These communities arrived on American shores uninfluenced and unadulterated by all the ages and stages between the North American Indian and the post-Renaissance European.

Five centuries later, in the Age of the Air, the twentieth-century Americans' Power to Leap was still more unprecedented. Aeronautics and electronics extended the reach of man's leap all over the earth and into the heavens. The time required to send a message across the planet was abbreviated until it became practically instantaneous. This was a quantum jump in technological progress.

Aeronautics and electronics obviously brought Americans much closer to the moon, but not any closer to their next-door neighbors. In surprising ways, the Power to Leap now tended to isolate and segregate each citizen from those nearby. This is an example of what I would call the Law of Inverted Distance: *Advancing technology tends to have a proportionately much greater effect on large quantities than on small.* The longer the distance to be covered, the greater the power of technology to reduce the required time. This means that within the short distances circumscribing man's everyday community, the distances that measure his neighborhood, the powers of this technology are negligible.

It is misleading, then, simply to say that when the "Space Age" came, space was "conquered." It would be more accurate to say that physical distance became an everyday conundrum. The electronic impulses which penetrated walls and hastened over thousands of miles also made a puzzle of everyday experience.

This new Power to Leap would have a profound effect on daily life, on the citizen's consciousness, on his relation to government and to nearly everything else. Suddenly every citizen was catapulted into a ringside seat in the national capital. Messages and images from Washington reached the citizen just as readily whether he was in San Francisco, Salt Lake City, or Miami Beach, on shipboard in the Great Lakes, or off Cape Cod. The large investment by the broadcasting networks in Washington and in New York made the programs from such centers superior both technically and in personnel to local broadcasts. Now every American, however far from Washington, could feel present at the Inauguration of a President, at the histrionics of Congressional Hearings, at the Press Conferences in the State Department or the White House.

Of course, the State Capitols and City Halls, too, were scenes of broadcasts. But the most important new influence of television on the American political consciousness was to give immediacy and intimacy to events and personalities *at a great distance.* Citizens who could not even name, much less recognize, their representative in the State legislature now had a casual familiarity with the voice, facial expressions and intimidating gestures of a Senator Joe McCarthy, or the twitching eyebrows and affable smile of a Senator Sam Ervin. Nightly network newscasters Howard K. Smith and Walter Cronkite became a new type of folk hero.

All over the country, Americans were still troubled as much as ever by the impurity of their local water supply, by the irregularity of the collection of their garbage, by the overcrowding of their schools, by the risks of robbery and mayhem on the streets. But the vistas of everyday life were not what they used to be. Distant events and distant leaders seemed so much nearer and more vivid than many closer, more neighborly events.

BY-PRODUCTS

This power to conquer distance tended to revise or abolish the circumstances on which Franklin and Jefferson and Madison had based their political wisdom. The conditions which had supported the Founding Fathers' hopes for the future of the Republic were transformed.

Technology homogenizes. The very same forces which abridged the continental distances also tended to dissolve the continental variety. As people all over the United States came closer to one another, they became less different from one another. When businessmen and labor leaders flew halfway across the continent for a few hours' conference and returned home the same day, the whole nation's ways of doing business were assimilated. National advertising and national television programming brought the same sales slogans and the same entertainment celebrities simultaneously to everybody. Powerful homogenizing forces produced new reasons to share Thoreau's mid-nineteenth-century doubts. "We are in great haste," he noted in *Walden* in 1854, "to construct a magnetic telegraph from Maine to Texas; but Maine and Texas, it may be, have nothing important to communicate." The more alike became the economy, the standard of living, the spoken language, the folklore, the music, and the literary culture of the nation's distant parts, the less was added to any American's experience by bringing him words and music and images from remote parts of the nation. What had happened to the variety in which Jefferson had such confidence, and which gave him such comfort— that "while frenzy and delusion like an epidemic, gained certain parts, the residue remained sound and untouched"? Was any part of the nation still immune to these powerful homogenizers?

Technology centralizes. The new technology required great investments of capital and new kinds of specialized know-how. The high cost and the homogenizing reach of the media put a premium on the celebrity-everything—the celebrity product, the celebrity entertainer, the celebrity newscaster. The celebrity was a person who was well known for his well-knownness. To judge political candidates or commercial products by the "recognition factor" meant that candidates, products, and broadcasters would be valued quantitatively. The cost of commercial advertising announcements and the salaries of television entertainers and newscasters depended on how many people they reached and how many they managed to keep listening. These high costs could be borne only by high-powered, centralized institutions, the best-financed political candidates, and the most widely used soaps and soups and automobiles and deodorants. Every advance in technology seemed to increase the power of the broadcasting networks. The three great networks headquartered in New York employed the best technology and the best talent. An incumbent President who could command them all at will had a new advantage. News now tended to become afferent and efferent—no longer mostly dispersed near where it was gathered but attracted to centers from which it was dispersed everywhere.

Technology isolates. When Alexander Graham Bell exhibited his telephone in 1876, the popular imagination was excited by its fantastic possibilities. The author of a popular song, "The Wondrous Telephone," then unwittingly forecast the consequences of radio and television:

> *You stay at home and listen*
> *To the lecture in the hall,*
> *And hear the strains of music*
> *From a fascinating ball!*

In the following century, every new advance of electronic technology—from the telephone to the radio to television—tended increasingly to isolate individual Americans and keep them at home. This was perhaps the most momentous unpredicted consequence of the new Power to Leap. The telephone made it possible to have a conversation with a person without seeing his face or being in his physical presence. Television finally made it possible to join others in experiencing almost anything while remaining physically separated from them. All by yourself in your own home, while you were lolling in your favorite armchair smoking a cigarette and drinking a can of beer, you could attend a political rally, hear a concert, observe a funeral or some other public ritual, or be present at a parade. Relaxed in your pajamas or nightgown as you lay in bed, you were free from the old rules of decorum. You were free from the need to stay silent, you could applaud or hiss, walk in late or walk out in the middle.

Why risk the traffic or endure the crowds for what would come home to you on your TV screen? Television thus brought a new personal isolation and spelled the decline of congregation.

Of course, millions of Americans still attended amateur school or church performances, patronized live theater or concerts, or paid their money to enjoy the living three-dimensional excitement of the baseball stands, the football stadium, or the hockey rink. But many more millions preferred the close-ups and the replays offered free-of-charge on the TV screen. Some of the best views of national political conventions were those that reached the citizens who had stayed home. As the evening audiences for downtown theaters declined, so too did all the other once-appealing features of "downtown." And "downtown" was diffused into indistinguishable shopping centers where branches of national retail chains were selling the same brands. The consumer went to the nearest one. For politics and entertainment, Americans tended to go out less than ever before, yet they were witnessing events occurring at a farther distance than ever before. The more Americans stayed at home, the more they found their attention focused on the faraway.

Television became a form of transportation. In fact, it was better than any earlier form of transportation. For it brought preselected, well-focused, telephoto versions of the most interesting aspects of any experience instantaneously from everywhere. The old technology took the person to the experience; the new technology brought the experience to the person.

No longer was it necessary to go out into the presence of numerous of your fellowmen to witness the most costly performances. Formerly the lavish extravaganzas brought out the biggest crowds, and even *had to* bring out the crowds to support the events. Now these were the very programs most likely to go direct to the greatest number of individuals, each at his receiver, each witnessing the performance in privacy. The biggest and best events tended to be witnessed-at-a-distance. The bigger and better the event, the greater the distance!

Television, then, produced a new segregation. And every advance in technology, every reduction in the cost of sets, every improvement in the quality of reception tended to increase the physical segregation of the individuals who shared an experience. When color television appeared, Americans did not dispose of their old black-and-white sets in order to bring the family together again before the color screen. Instead, the black-and-white set was given to the children for their room, while the color set moved into the adults' living room. Small, inexpensive sets made it possible for more members of the family to have their very own screen and watch their favorite programs all by themselves. More Americans could buy portable sets and take the screen with them—to the beach, the mountains, or the campsite—and so isolate themselves from the landscape they had gone to see.

A similar tendency to isolation came along with the advancing technology of transportation. The Pilgrim Fathers on their voyage across the ocean had been packaged together in a shipboard community, and as they lived in forced intimacy for weeks, they grew into a seagoing village. Contrast this with the experience of the twentieth-century transatlantic traveler, who is urged to keep his seat belt constantly fastened. He is saved from the need to converse with fellow passengers by the headset which brings him a private concert or a humorous monologuist. For most of that few hours' voyage he need not see his fellow passengers, since the lights are dimmed for better viewing of the motion-picture screen.

Even before the airplane, the automobile had a similar atomizing effect. Traveling by train had been a social experience. In the nineteenth century, the characteristic open design of American railroad cars—unlike the closed compartments of the British or the continental cars—developed out of the Americans' desire to move about and mix with fellow passengers. The Pullman smoking room became a fertile source of American folklore. Those Americans who still commuted by train continued to have the friendly experience of waiting with their neighbors on the station platform, of conversing or playing cards, or even drinking a cocktail en route.

But the automobile was isolating and encapsulating. The American traveling to work by car was apt to be traveling alone, probably listening to his radio for music or news from some distant center. Car pools made little headway even in an age of gas shortages. The improved American highway system still further isolated the American-in-transit. On his speedway—identified only by a highway number, graded, landscaped, and fenced, with not so much as a stoplight to interrupt his passage—he had no contact with the towns which he by-passed. If he stopped for food or gas, he was served no local fare or local fuel, but had one of Howard Johnson's nationally branded ice cream flavors, and so many gallons of Exxon. This vast ocean of superhighways was nearly as free of culture as the sea traversed by the *Mayflower* Pilgrims. Just as television now tended to keep every man by himself at home, the automobile meant every man for himself on the road.

Meanwhile, technology tended to clog the short-distance channels. Americans found it difficult to accommodate traditional neighborhoods to the needs of the new machines. The automobile, which had the capacity to cruise at sixty miles an hour, seemed at first to give man a new Power to Leap on land. But around cities, where short-distance transportation was crucial, automobile passengers were often confined in traffic jams where they could not even progress at a walking pace. The shorter the distance, the larger the Parking Problem. In fact, parking began to rank with the dilemmas of sex and politics, death and taxes as the common lot of humankind—the most modern symbol of the Fall of Man. The automobile proved to be an effective time-saver only for longer distances, where it did not block the channels of its own passage.

The airplane would provide another example. It had made Daedalus' dream into an everyday reality. Habits and institutions changed as the airplane abridged large distances. Businessmen headquartered in Chicago transacted daily business in Los Angeles or New York. Baseball leagues no longer had to be concentrated in one part of the country—the Brooklyn Dodgers moved to California to become the Los Angeles

Dodgers, and the American League spread across the continent.

Again the Law of Inverted Distance was at work. Airplane schedules had to include a factor for the traffic jam. When it took less than an hour to fly the 213 miles from National Airport in Washington to LaGuardia Airport in New York, it might take as long or longer by car to traverse the eight miles from LaGuardia Airport to midtown Manhattan. Bigger planes required metropolitan airports to be located at ever greater distances from the city center. Several cities, such as Dallas and Fort Worth, shared a single equidistant airport. To avoid the travail of short-distance transportation, intercity meetings were held in the hotels right at the airport. But the multiplying airplanes, like the multiplying automobiles, also could clog their channels in the air. It was not uncommon to spend two hours flying the thousand miles from Chicago to Atlanta, then spend a half-hour circling in sight of the airport before air traffic control gave the clearance to land.

DISTANCE LOSES ITS FORCE

In this curious upside-down world, men could leap the long distances in speed and comfort, yet they were more than ever cursed by the perils and congestions of short distances. What did this do to the therapy of remoteness? In the founding era, many of the special opportunities of American civilization had arisen from the fact that the long distances—between the Old World and the New, between one end of the colonies and

the other, between one side of the continent and the other—
were still intractable and still appeared unconquerable by
any speedy means. This helped explain why Americans who
were so far from the British Isles had established self-government, while the inhabitants of nearby Ireland had not, and
why London monopolists could not enforce their privileges
across the Atlantic. Simple remoteness explained countless
American opportunities.

But those twentieth-century successes of American technology which brought people all over the United States
closer to one another also made them less different from one
another. New problems and new confusions came along with
new benefits and opportunities. The tendency of modern
industry to congregate workers in ever-larger factories had
long been noted. In the early nineteenth century, Karl Marx
shrewdly predicted that this fact might give a new self-consciousness, a new sense of community, and a new power to
those who worked together. What Marx could not foresee
(and what few Americans in the twentieth century noted)
was that the ever-wider diffusion of the products of American factories tended toward the increasing isolation of con-
sumers from one another. It was not just that Rebecca no
longer went to the village well for her water—and her gossip.
She no longer needed to go outside her kitchenette apartment
to have her hot and cold running water, her hot and cold
running entertainment. Even her garbage no longer had to
be carried out, for the waste food went into the Disposall,
while papers, cans, and bottles went into the trash compac-
tor.

Was it any wonder that the troubles of American cities
multiplied beyond measure? American city-dwellers were

not backward in complaining of crime on the streets, of the inadequacy of municipal services and of public transportation. Yet they seemed unable to bring their energies and ingenuities to bear on these problems which harassed them every day and every night, right where they lived.

Was it possible to restore the therapy of distance? Were there antidotes for the technological segregation of individuals? What could be done to prevent splendid technology from breeding a menacing personal isolationism? Was there any way of using the new Power to Leap so as to restore the neighborliness of the near?

V

THE DARK CONTINENT
OF TECHNOLOGY:
☆ THE ENLARGED ☆
CONTEMPORARY

Thomas Jefferson is best known for the Declaration of Independence, in which he announced the separation of the
thirteen British Colonies in North America—the right of
Americans in these places to govern themselves. He should
also be known for declaring another kind of Independence,
the sovereignty of the people living at any one time over their
own affairs. We have seen that he urged Americans to "consider each generation as a distinct nation, with a right, by the
will of its majority, to bind themselves, but none to bind the
succeeding generation, more than the inhabitants of another
country." And he added: "The dead have no rights. They are
nothing; and nothing cannot own something. . . . This corporeal globe, and everything upon it, belongs to its present
corporeal inhabitants, during their generation." This way of

thinking gave Jefferson's generation the courage to do the unprecedented—to found a new nation.

In our time we have had revealed to us a new and wider meaning for Jefferson's principle of the sovereignty of the present generation. The sovereign present has become the imperial present, dominating our knowledge and our concerns, reaching out with menacing power over vast areas of our consciousness.

We have seen how aeronautics and electronics gave to *spatial* dimensions a disorienting new irrelevance. Americans, unsure whether what they viewed on television was actually happening in Chicago, Los Angeles, or New York, or in a nearby studio, were newly uncertain about the *where* of events. They would be no less confused about the *when*. Candid photography, the hand-held motion-picture camera, the novel powers of kinescoping and videotaping—all these would affect the viewer's sense of time with a new ambiguity. Was what you watched actually happening while you watched, had it been filmed an hour—a week, or a year—before, or was it a "rerun" of something made last season? A new chronological fog enshrouded the television experience, which, of course, became an ever-increasing, ever more dominant proportion of everyone's experience. By the mid-1970's, the best estimates suggested that an American spent, on the average, six hours a day at the television screen. The dimensions of this confusion were betrayed in a new meaning attached to "life" itself, when Americans commonly asked themselves, "This thing that I'm watching—is it 'live'?"

THE ISTHMUS OF THE PRESENT

While philosophers describe the "present" as nothing more than a fleeting moment, in common experience we cannot help feeling that the present has dimensions. As the Irish poet Thomas Moore observed, the present is

> *A narrow isthmus 'twixt two boundless seas,*
> *The past, the future, two eternities.*

Many facts of life—including our technology—make the isthmus of the present seem either narrow or wide. How we see the dimensions of the present depends on the reach and sharpness and vividness of our vision.

In our vision of items extended through *space,* we Americans have developed a kind of far-sightedness. An ophthalmologist might say that we suffer from *Hyperopia,* a pathological condition in which vision is better for distant than for near objects. In our chronological vision, our sense of *time,* we Americans have come to suffer from an opposite disorder, a kind of near-sightedness. This is a form of *Myopia,* a pathological condition in which the nearby is clear but the distant is blurred and hard to discern.

In other words, we have enlarged our sense of the contemporary. We are overwhelmed by our sense of where we, and our contemporaries all over the world, are at this moment. Improved communications are obviously the most potent of the forces that overwhelm us with impressions of the now. And there are many others.

More and more of what we Americans wear, buy, live in,

and display on our persons and in our houses are recently produced. Of course, we still have our wealthy collectors of Old Masters and a lively cult of antique buffs. But for most Americans the heirloom has become a disappearing phenomenon. Objects that elsewhere might be valued as antique we are inclined to call secondhand. In other times and places, the most valuable inheritance was the ancestral home. But, in the United States, who wants to live in his father's—much less his grandfather's—house? Upward-mobile Americans might not even want to live in that neighborhood! In the late twentieth century, in fashionable magazines like *The New Yorker,* advertisements for diamonds which once had promised "Diamonds are for Ever" have been revised to read, "Diamonds are for Now."

For two centuries, American mobility has required a willingness—sometimes it has been an eagerness—to leave things behind. Moving westward, across the Atlantic or across the continent, meant learning to travel light. And that meant separating yourself from the treasures, as well as the land, of your ancestors. In the diaries of the early nineteenth-century wagon trains, we hear a common refrain: the housewife's lament at what could not be brought along.

Our technology, oddly enough, has made it more difficult than ever to transport objects through the expanses of time. The contagion of the annual model infects almost everything we wear or use. I happen to possess a gold pocket-watch which was given to my father when he became Worshipful Master of his Masonic Lodge in 1913. It was intended to become an heirloom, like the proverbial gold-watch award for the man who has given fifty years of service to his firm. But the awarding of such watches has become increasingly rare—and not only because fewer people nowadays spend fifty years with the same company.

In the United States, our watches—like everything else—express an annual-model technology. The gold case of my father's watch must be opened to set the hands, and there is a prominent stem for winding. I am no connoisseur of time-pieces and yet in recent years I have moved up from an old-fashioned self-winder to an electronic Accutron, and finally to a digital quartzomatic. Timex, an American firm and reputedly the world's largest maker of watches, and other American manufacturers have persuaded us to buy watches to go with this year's frock, and hopefully to go out of fashion just as quickly. We have sports watches, watches for business wear or for dinner wear, with changeable bands and changeable faces. In textiles, too, where for centuries people had to choose among cotton, linen, wool, and silk, our products have become kaleidoscopic. When we buy this year's cut of the collar, we must decide whether to take it in nylon, dacron, viyella, lycra, acetate, quiana, or some other fabric that may not even be available next year.

The corruption of obsolescence has actually given novel appeal to works of art as items of investment. An item bought as a cold-blooded investment is not apt to become an heirloom. We might emend the Biblical caution to read, "Lay not up for yourselves treasures upon earth, where everything becomes obsolete."

The high cost of labor and the constant development of new plastics has led to the "disposable" everything. Each time we throw away a paper napkin or a plastic coffee cup, we discard another tiny link from today to yesterday.

The new perfections of communication which have climaxed in twentieth-century America do not succeed in conquering *time*, however successful they have been in conquering *space*. The telegraph, the telephone, radio, and television take messages and images across the continent but they cannot cross the centuries. This simple obvious fact, momentous for our American sense of time, helps account for our enlarged sense of the contemporary.

Even before our day of electronics, the improved American technology of communication had shown the same tendency, and the same limitations. The mass-circulating newspaper (facilitated by the telegraph and the telephone) after the middle of the nineteenth century was to become the overwhelming new force in the American public consciousness. Now Chicagoans at their breakfast tables could be informed of events of the last few hours, whether these had occurred in Washington or New York, Los Angeles or San Francisco, London or Tokyo.

The multiplying daily papers were intended to be a report and not a record. Today's newspaper had to become obsolete to clear the market for tomorrow's. All over the world, newspapers multiplied. In Britain, for example, after the newspaper tax was repealed in 1855, the number of newspapers trebled in forty years. In the United States, this increase was astronomical, expanding from a daily newspaper circulation of 758,000 in 1850 to 15,102,000 in 1900. The increased demand for paper could no longer be satisfied by linen and cotton rags and straw, the main raw materials until then in use. This demand was met through new techniques for making paper by boiling wood chips with soda or sulfite solutions. By 1890, most of the world's paper was being made in this way. Wood pulp provided endless quantities of paper in rolls two miles long to feed the speed presses which brought today's news from everywhere to everybody.

By a malign providence, this very technology which succeeded in keeping the avenues of communication open through space has clogged the highways of time. Within a few decades, it was discovered that the abundant new wood-pulp paper would not survive the passage of years. By mid-twentieth century, the billions of wood-pulp pages were turning brown and brittle. The books of the modern world were falling apart. To be preserved to posterity they would have to be put in some other form. The paper-making technology which had been improved to inform a literate democracy became a menace. Unless librarians and publishers acted promptly, the literary culture of modern times, along with the spoken words of earlier generations, would be gone-with-the-wind. In a single recent year (1970), the Library of Congress microfilmed some 2,200,658 disintegrating pages of modern books. Yet this was less than one-quarter of one percent of the volumes in its collections which were known to be turning to dust. In addition to the cost, there was the troublesome necessity for librarians to play God. They had to decide which of the past century's books ought to command the attention of the future.

A similar malign providence seemed to preside over the birth of motion pictures. The nitrate film on which early American motion pictures were recorded was not only inflammable but explosive. This required another costly and complicated effort (again at the Library of Congress, and under the auspices of the American Film Institute)—to transfer the works of Douglas Fairbanks, Mary Pickford, Charlie Chaplin, and countless others from the dangerous

nitrate film to safety film. Otherwise, many of the first classics of our great democratic art would be lost to the next
generation. Our television networks film brilliant reports of
the exciting events of our time, but most such films and
kinescope tapes are erased or destroyed. Unless someone
takes the initiative for their preservation, they will not become records for the future.

In our age, then, communication seldom means the trans-
mission of messages from one time to another. Although
there has never before been a generation that sent so many
messages to itself, we are tragically inept at receiving messages from our ancestors or sending messages to our posterity. Much of what passes for "communication" has become
simply another way of reminding us of the here-and-now.
Every day we are flooded with disposable memoranda from
us to ourselves.

THE THERAPY OF DELAY

So long as the only vehicle for diffusing news was the printed
page, there was always a gap of at least several hours between
when something happened and when people far from the
scene got the word. It took time to prepare a report and get
it from the site of the event to the waiting citizens. On the
countryside or off the beaten track, they might have to wait
days or weeks, depending on the state of the roads and the
efficiency of delivery.

American history is full of instances of how the considerable time required to transmit a message from one place to
another shaped the course of events. The nation itself was

vast, and an ocean separated it from the capitals of Europe where crucial history-making decisions had to be made.

For example, if in 1803 there had been speedy communications between Paris and Washington, the Louisiana Purchase (which doubled the size of the nation and extended the United States westward to the Rocky Mountains and beyond) might never have been made. President Thomas Jefferson had instructed his emissaries to purchase enough land at the mouth of the Mississippi River to assure free navigation by Americans and the use of the port for transshipment of goods. When Napoleon surprised the American delegation by offering the vast Louisiana Territory at a bargain price, he demanded a quick reply. If James Monroe, Jefferson's special envoy, and Robert R. Livingston, then the United States Minister in Paris, had been able to consult their capital, it is more than likely that President Jefferson and the Congress would have balked. For Jefferson had made a political principle of construing the Constitution strictly, and the Constitution had given no clear authority for such additions to the national territory. But without delay, and without consulting their capital, Monroe and Livingston struck the bargain on their own. Faced not with the question but with the answer, Jefferson put his constitutional scruples behind him, and Congress ratified what they would not have initiated.

On another occasion, the lack of a technology of haste actually helped prevent war between the United States and Great Britain. On November 8, 1861, a few months after the outbreak of the American Civil War between the northern Union and the southern Confederacy, Captain Charles Wilkes of the Union Navy ship *San Jacinto* boarded and searched the British mail steamer *Trent* and took off the two Confederate Agents who were then en route to Paris. In the United States, the Secretary of the Navy congratulated Wilkes for his "great public service," and the House of Representatives even voted him a gold medal. The British public, meanwhile, clamored for war against the United States because of this violation of British rights on the high seas. "There never was within memory such a burst of feeling," an English observer noted. "The people are frantic with rage, and were the country polled, I fear 999 men out of a thousand would declare for immediate war." The British government sent 8,000 troops to defend Canada, and forbade the export of arms to America.

Some time before this episode, the American Secretary of War, William H. Seward, had expressed his quixotic hope for a war with some European power. Such an outside threat, he argued, could not substantially damage the United States, and yet would very likely solidify the nation, bring the errant Southern States back into the Union, and so end the Civil War. "If the Lord would only give the United States," he prayed, "an excuse for a war with England, France, or Spain!" The *Trent* affair looked like Seward's God-given opportunity. And if there had been a submarine cable across the Atlantic during those early November days, the *Trent* affair easily could have become the occasion for war between Great Britain and the United States.

Happily, there was time for the therapy of delay. On the American side, Seward, counseled by the cautious President Lincoln, had time to reconsider, and in Britain, too, there were weeks for passions to cool. The prudent Charles Francis Adams, American Minister in London, was given the opportunity to develop his personal understanding with the British Foreign Minister, Lord Russell, and to palliate public antipa- thies. The United States government, finally convinced that Captain Wilkes had violated the established practice of the seas, on December 26 "cheerfully liberated" the Confederate agents. But if Britain had joined the Confederacy's war against the Union the struggle surely would have been lengthened and the outcome might have been different.

Geographic distance, which in those days meant remote- ness, gave American diplomats on the distant scene the op- portunity for reflection. An ambassador was more likely to be an active agent of decision. The public, too, was less tempted to act precipitately.

The rise of instantaneous communication, the ubiquity of radio and television, and the intrusion of media into private and public vehicles, into living rooms and public places, today reduce whatever chance there once might have been for the therapy of delay. The high cost of publishing or broadcasting increases pressure to get *some*thing into print or on the air, and speedily. Often, even before the reporter can find out precisely what he is talking about, and surely before he has had time to reflect, or to examine the event's context and/or its significance.

The printed page required some person to *translate* the event into words. What reached the reader was not the event itself but the reporter's account. Photography changed this to a degree, but so long as the photographer was limited to a single shot of an event or to a few newspaper columns, he, too, was essentially an interpreter.

In our electronic age, the pressures and the trend are all in the other direction. The special virtues of the new media are speed, immediacy, and vividness. More and more "reports" of news are actual views of the events and the actors. The "documentary" news "reporter" no longer needs to translate the event into words, or to translate somebody else's colloquial expressions into journalese. Much of the "reporter's" effort goes to manipulate the machinery (sometimes the actors themselves), to ensure proper lighting, to see that there are enough different cameras set at the proper angles—so that we can witness the unmediated event. We view the actor in the event at the very scene of action. He has just had a microphone thrust in his face, and he tells us how it seems to him. *Eyewitness News! You Are There!*

THE NEED FOR ERASURE: THE RECEDING PAST

American journalism had unwittingly provided every American with what Pliny called "proof of opulence, and . . . quite the glory of luxury, to possess that which may be irremediably destroyed in an instant." Every day—every few hours—television viewers were offered a costly news-product which might become worthless in a few hours, and was almost certain to lose its interest in a few days. Only by making today's product obsolete would tomorrow's product seem necessary. The news appeared in new models hourly. A well-informed citizen was expected to discard the seven o'clock model for that which appeared only three hours later.

This brought a newly urgent need—the need for *Erasure.* An ever-larger proportion of the older model of news had to be erased to make way for the up-to-the-minute. Unmediated accounts now were sent out before the "reporter" had an opportunity to educate himself on the subject. Was "Diego García" a man, a country, a political party—or perhaps a cigar? Inevitably, every account required correction, addition, subtraction, revision. The more instantaneous the communication, the wider the diffusion of news, the greater the need for erasure. Every act of erasure was costly, and required as much technology as the original broadcast. The erasure itself became a way of reinforcing the recent.

Radio and television broadcasting measured messages by the minute and the hour. The repetitious pattern of advertising "news" somehow froze a pattern for all other kinds. News reporting on the hour or the half-hour—when only part of the earlier news had been obsoleted—meant a great deal of repetition. I cannot recall any significant news event that I ever heard broadcast only once. The eleven o'clock news repeats the main items (sometimes the whole program) of the ten o'clock news, the ten o'clock news repeats items from the seven o'clock news, and so on.

When the news came packaged in newspapers, you were free to decide when or whether you would open the package, and you could refuse to read the item again. But television is another story. You can't scan the item before you read it. You can't know what new calamity you might be missing or what the breathless reporter might be about to describe. You become a victim of repetition even as you try to focus your TV vision on something really new. Such repetition, reinforcing the recent, becomes another device for enlarging the contemporary.

No wonder, then, that we have a new hierarchy of interpreters. We need them not only to tell us what must be erased from yesterday's news, but also to guide us through the fast-growing thicket of today. Back in the archaic age, the Age of Again-and-Again, when the principal human concern was for the return of the familiar, for ensuring the cycle of the seasons, the high priests were the masters of magic and religion, the priest-kings and the king-priests. They had the power to preserve the regularity of events. In the next age, the Age of History, the heroes were statesmen and men of science, innovators in thought and institutions, discoverers and inventors, or even historians—those who *made* the authentically new or who recorded it.

In our age—an Age of the Enlarged Contemporary— those to whom we turn for meaning are the Newsmen. They tell us what to make of the current flood of information and sensations. The increase of unmediated reports increases our need for interpretation. If not at the very moment when we first get the report, as soon thereafter as possible. We have our parish priests (the local television news reporters), our bishops, and even our cardinals (the network "anchormen").

While the distant in space comes to us effortlessly in our living rooms, the distant in time recedes from our view. Our wide-angle lens encompasses vast territories of the recent and the far away within the contemporary. Nearly everything that comes to us from the past—not only in our books and magazines, but even in our schools and colleges—is sifted through the sieve of relevance. The lead review in our most widely circulating literary medium, the *New York Times Book Review,* must be "newsworthy"—tied somehow to current events. Our elaborate audio-visual aids themselves confine us within the peculiar concerns of our own age. We all become more and more like the old lady in Boston, Massachusetts, who was asked whether she traveled much.

"No," she answered, "why should I? I'm already there." Just as we prefer to stay home and see it on television, so we find it more comfortable to sit in our own century and be reminded of ourselves.

Despite our facilities for all other forms of travel, we find ourselves peculiarly ill-equipped and ill-disposed to travel back through time. When we go there, we are inclined to see everything with the fashionable myopia of our age. We look for materials to teach the place of Women in History, materials for Black Studies, or data on what we pretentiously call "the Environment." The past, which should be the Land of the Otherwise, opening our imagination to possibilities not visible in our time and place, becomes a Land of the More-So, which we plunder to document what we already believe.

The paper record of the recent and the current becomes an overwhelming flood. It is estimated that the 31,000,000 pages preserved from the administrations of President Lyndon Johnson actually exceed the manuscript collections on all the Presidents before the Twentieth century. The gargantuan archives of the recent become a barrier between us and the more remote past. Our anxious efforts to enlarge the contemporary create a penumbra which is not quite the present, but not yet discarded to history.

"The Generation Gap," once taken for granted, was a gulf across which the older generation passed its knowledge. Education was once equated with acculturation, while acculturation was equated with society's ways of inducting the young into the accumulated wisdom. But as more and more of our valued knowledge is of a scientific or socially contemporary character, knowledge is confused with information, and it too becomes quickly obsolete. Not so long ago, we American parents were teaching our children the multiplication table, but nowadays we turn to our children to learn of the New Math, the New Physics, and the Language of Computers. Abraham Lincoln grew a beard before he ran for President to give him the dignity of age, but now the white-haired elder statesman is out of fashion. A United States Senator may grow a beard to seem youthful, or he may dye his hair to remove tell-tale traces of gray. What we find in the twentieth-century United States is not so much a Generation Gap as a Generation Blur!

In the early centuries of American life, the New World wondered how to seize the unprecedented opportunities for visible beginnings, for ways to start over, to break with the past. In the late twentieth century, we face a quite different, but just as urgent problem: how to keep in touch with the past. Not just the patriotic American past, but the whole human past. How to remind ourselves that we live not only among contemporaries, but in the whole stream of human-kind on our planet.

The accelerating pace of scientific progress is another name for the quick obsolescence of knowledge. What Americans of my generation learned in school as physics or chemistry is now data only for the historian of science. "The importance of a scientific work," the eminent German mathematician David Hilbert observed, "can be measured by the number of previous publications it makes superfluous to read." Books and articles with the power to obsolesce their predecessors tumble in on us every day. Scientists on the frontiers of knowledge—and there are tens of thousands in the United States today—no longer dare await the printed word to learn of the progress in their field. They rely increasingly on the telephone, or on Telex, and they are airborne to frequent conferences drawing together their colleagues from long distances.

The great works of science inevitably bury their predecessors, and the best science fiction becomes obsolete by the fulfillment of its prophecies. But the great works of literature, of history, of philosophy, and of speculation enrich and revive their predecessors. As T. S. Eliot explained in his essay "Tradition and the Individual Talent," every great writer has the magical power—if only we can see it—of deepening and broadening the meaning of all those who came before. But our Age of the Enlarged Contemporary is tempted to assign the "irrelevant" past to the junk heap of the obsolete. The din of the contemporary drowns out the quiet voices of the past.

Even as we in the United States progress in our efforts to enlarge our democracy, to give voice to those who have been denied, we have unwittingly disfranchised countless others. For, as G. K. Chesterton in *Orthodoxy* observed:

> Tradition may be defined as an extension of the franchise.
> Tradition means giving votes to the most obscure of all classes,
> our ancestors. It is the democracy of the dead. Tradition
> refuses to submit to the small and arrogant oligarchy of those
> who merely happen to be walking about. All democrats object
> to men being disqualified by the accident of birth; tradition
> objects to their being disqualified by the accident of death.
> Democracy tells us not to neglect a good man's opinion, even
> if he is our groom; tradition asks us not to neglect a good
> man's opinion, even if he is our father. . . . the two ideas of
> democracy and tradition . . . are the same idea. We will have
> the dead at our councils. The ancient Greeks voted by stones;

these shall vote by tombstones. It is all quite regular and official, for most tombstones, like most ballot papers, are marked with a cross.

The progress of communications in the United States has created new problems of communication—of communication with those nearby in space, of communication with those remote from us in time.

VI

THE FUTURE
☆ OF EXPLORATION ☆

The New World entered the consciousness of the Old World with the modern birth of Exploration. The distinction between *discovery* (locating something you knew was there) and *exploring* (encountering and wandering through the unknown) helps us understand how the American experience has added to the World Experience. If the United States is to continue to play its catalytic role in the world, if it is to continue to stir mankind to the impossible, we must keep alive and socialize the exploring spirit. This is not easy. Great forces at work since the founding of our nation have tempted us to give up our exploring—or to leave it to marginal men and women. But I will suggest some of the ways of thinking, the frame of mind, which may help us keep that spirit alive.

THE GREAT COINCIDENCE:
SCIENCE AND DEMOCRACY

In the later twentieth century, the whole world—and especially the people of the United States—has been the beneficiary of two modern, world-shaping movements: the Scientific Movement, and the Democratic Movement. Both have been gathering force during the four and a half centuries since the first European settlements of North America. The great Scientific Movement goes back to Copernicus and Sir Francis Bacon and Galileo. With it came a new emphasis on natural laws, on prediction, on the gathering of facts, on measurement, and on precision. The great Democratic Movement, which goes back to Martin Luther, Oliver Cromwell, and John Locke, brought a new emphasis on the power and wisdom of the people. The common denominator of the two modern movements has been a tendency to distrust tradition and authority. Historians, therefore, have commonly lumped the two movements together under some such name as the Enlightenment, the Age of Reason, or the Rise of Liberalism.

The Scientific Movement revealed a new reach of man's knowledge. Sir Isaac Newton proved that God was a mathematician, and that man could grasp the Divine mathematics.

Nature and nature's laws lay hid in night:
God said, Let Newton be! and all was light.

So Alexander Pope rhapsodized in his Epitaph for Newton (1730) in Westminster Abbey. No wonder that when Newton's work was popularized the prestige of scientists increased. As Charles Churchill, an eighteenth-century radical, champion of John Wilkes, debunker of Dr. Johnson and other pillars of tradition, boasted:

> And Newton, something more than man,
> Div'd into nature's hidden springs,
> Laid bare the principles of things,
> Above the earth our spirits bore,
> And gave us worlds unknown before.

The word "science" (which till then had meant all human knowledge) took on a sharp new meaning. Now it was both a description of what man knew and a demonstration of a new-found mastery of the universe. By 1840, the mathematician William Whewell had introduced the word "scientist" in its modern sense. The scientist became the high priest of the new age.

Dazzled by the sudden and spectacular growth of knowledge through science, we are tempted to forget that the rise of science was also a new recognition of the extent of the unknown. Newton, who always remained something of a mystic, did not share the complacent pride which he had engendered. "I do not know what I may appear to the world," he wrote near the end of his life, "but to myself I seem to have been only like a boy playing on the seashore, and diverting myself in now and then finding a smoother pebble or a prettier shell than ordinary, whilst the great ocean of truth lay all undiscovered before me."

Modern science was born in man's vision of this ocean of ignorance. It was born in the Exploring Spirit. The great scientists were also Negative Discoverers. They helped mankind see how little was yet known. They pointed the way to new Americas of the mind, realms of ignorance never before imagined to be there.

The modern Democratic Movement, too, conceived in bold acts of Negative Discovery, was also born with the Exploring Spirit. Anointed kings and hereditary aristocrats, professors and popes and priests—all these were proved to be much less wise than had been believed. New ways of thinking dissipated the "divinity that doth hedge a king." Democracy brought into politics a Newtonian awe of "the great ocean of truth . . . all undiscovered." It socialized the exploring spirit, keeping it alive for future generations of explorers.

During the very years when the people of Western Europe were acquiring their reverence for the powers of science, they were awakened to the ignorance and hypocrisy of priests and monarchs. Thomas Paine found the origin of Monarchy in the victory of a "banditti of Ruffians" who had overrun the country and laid it under contribution and "the chief of the band contrived to lose the name of Robber in that of Monarch, and hence the origin of Monarchy and Kings." Jefferson saw the wolves pretending to guard the sheep. "It seems to be the law of our general nature," he observed in Paris in 1787, "in spite of individual exceptions; and experience declares that man is the only animal which devours his own kind; for I can apply no milder term to the governments of Europe, and to the general prey of the rich on the poor."

Only the alertness of the whole people could save them from exploitation. "Cherish, therefore, the spirit of our people, and keep alive their attention. Do not be too severe upon their errors, but reclaim them by enlightening them. If once they become inattentive to public affairs, you and I, and Congress and Assemblies, Judges and Governors, shall all become wolves."

Modern democracy, then, was not conceived in any naïve belief in the people's omniscience—rather in a skepticism of what had long passed for virtue and knowledge. It was born less in faith than in doubt. It was a refuge from Old Pretenders. This was the deeper wisdom in Sir Winston Churchill's quip that Democracy is not a good form of government, but only better than all other known forms. The best prophets of democracy did not sing paeans of praise to the people, but enlisted all in a common voyage of exploration—away from an Old World of known evils, toward a New World of experiment.

It is not surprising that demagogues, the experts in rhetorical overkill, have claimed divine virtues for the people and divine wisdom for their majority will. But the oft-quoted obscurantist maxim *vox populi, vox Dei* ("the voice of the people is the voice of God") is medieval and not modern. It comes from the eighth century before such nonsense had been disproved by experience. The great democratic philosophers, especially in the United States, have defended popular government as a protective device, a way of keeping the people alert to the weakness, dishonesty, and pretentiousness of their rulers, a way of keeping alive the popular will to experiment.

THE IDEA OF NEGATIVE DISCOVERY

The so-called Enlightenment emphasized the extent and not the limits of knowledge. Such complacency brought with it a profoundly misleading (and illiberal) assumption: that progress consists only in enlarging our positive knowledge. But the advance of the human spirit must also be measured by our increasing awareness of our ignorance. "Knowledge," as George Santayana observed, "is recognition of something absent; it is a salutation, not an embrace." Any awakening to another area or another dimension of our ignorance is what I call a Negative Discovery. It enlarges our self-awareness. The so-called "Discovery" of America—the modern parable of the Exploring Spirit—is my prototype of Negative Discovery.

The prophets of the Exploring Spirit include others, of course, besides the Magellans, the Amerigo Vespuccis, the Captain Cooks—the explorers of our physical planet. They must include the adventurers into science and social science, into the inner world of the human consciousness, and even into the world of dreams. Among them we must surely count such men as Charles Darwin, Karl Marx, and Sigmund Freud. They, too, revealed new areas of our ignorance. Darwin, wandering the dark continent of genetics, showed that we did not know as much as we thought we knew about the origin of species. Marx, ranging the dark continent of economics, revealed that we did not know as much as we thought we knew about the processes of history and the forces of politics. Freud, plunging into the dark continent of the subconscious, revealed that we did not know as much as we thought we knew about our own motives and feelings. While each of them began as a discoverer, they live on as explorers. Their enduring greatness was not as system-builders but as Negative Discoverers.

A free society is the natural habitat of the Negative Discoverer. In a censorship state, people are not free to discover the ignorance of their rulers, of their scientists, of their economists, of their priests—or of themselves. If they must sing paeans to the wisdom of their rulers, they dare not be rallied into the unknown. When force punishes the courageous few thousand who refuse to be censored, then acquiescent millions are frightened into censoring themselves. They are cowed into suppressing their awareness of their ignorance.

In our free United States, in our time, the forces which dull the exploring spirit happen to be by-products of progress—of the sciences and of our efforts to perfect democracy.

The Social Science Sieve: Boxing in the Future. The social sciences, employing the jargon of statistics, have become the sciences of social prophecy. Unlike the Delphic Oracle, these modern oracles actually consult the people. Market-researchers advise manufacturers and distributors on what the people want and what will sell. Opinion-researchers and opinion-pollsters tell voters the probable outcome of their future voting. One American opinion-researcher has even begun to supply expert predictions of the form and content of the predictions which will be made by other opinion-researchers. The sieve of social science sifts out the casual and the skew. The unpredictable unknown (if no longer terrifying as in the Age of Again-and-Again) is shunned. The future—once a reservoir of mystery—is confined within margins of error. Knowledge is tested by its usefulness for prediction. The social scientist becomes a new breed of social navigator, skilled at boxing in the future.

The Sieve of Relevance: Boxing in the Past. There has been a remarkable continuity to the American emphasis in education. The classics, according to Jefferson's friend, the pioneer American physician Benjamin Rush, were "as useless in America, as the Spanish great-coat is in the island of Cuba, or the Dutch foot-stove, at the Cape of Good Hope." He explained:

> We occupy a new country. Our principal business should be to explore and apply its resources, all of which press us to enterprize and haste. Under these circumstances, to spend four or five years in learning two dead languages, is to turn our backs upon a gold mine . . . to amuse ourselves in catching butterflies.

This American passion for relevance has never been sated. In the later nineteenth century, our proliferating Land Grant Colleges—the colleges founded from grants of federal lands —were devoted to the agricultural and mechanical arts, to home economics and the practical training of housewives and farmers. In the twentieth century, we have spent billions trying to bring "higher" education within the interests and capacities of every citizen, regardless of his actual interests or capacities. By 1975, student enrollment in American institutions of higher learning had exceeded ten million. "Relevance" has remained our watchword. The arts and literature, all the wisdom and learning of the past, are strained through the sieve of relevance. Popular educators—aided by parents, legislators, and students—try to ensure that whatever a student learns is not too surprising for him. They try to save students from the shock of the Otherwise. Curricula are planned to avoid adventures into the remote past, into the unfamiliar present, into the unknown or the dubiously productive. Just as social scientists box in the future, so educators box in the past.

The Sieve of Professionalism. British civilization has been blessed by a wholesome amateurism. But American civilization, which in the earliest age was characterized by the ingenious Yankee and the jack-of-all-trades, in the later twentieth century has been afflicted by a cancerous professionalism. The original remoteness of the American wilderness tended to turn the ancient and pompous learned professions into practical occupations open to all comers. By the later twentieth century we had turned the practical occupations into learned and pompous professions, and we had become the most professionalized nation in the world.

My own profession of historian is an example. A glory of English historical scholarship has been its amateur spirit—the passion of the lover who pursues his subject simply because he cannot resist its charms. In Britain, at least by American standards, there are relatively few professional societies for historians, and those give ample room to the amateur. In the United States, the contrast is striking. Historians, unabashed professionals, in numerous specialized societies hold annual meetings to which members fly across the continent. There the members may read and discuss scholarly papers in the conference rooms, but the real work is done in the corridors where they are concerned with professional matters like the job market. A proliferating professionalism separates us, and traditional academic categories of political history, diplomatic history, and economic history become pigeonholes. Even "interdisciplinary" categories such as Psycho-History and Quantitative History (so-called "Cliometrics") become self-conscious professional specialties. Vast areas—including, for example, most of the history of daily life (of food, shelter, and clothing)—remain beyond the pale. As a consequence, many of the most interesting topics in the American past await some maverick Negative Discoverer.

Minority Veto. In the mid-twentieth century, the United States underwent a Renaissance of Conscience. A passion for justice, a determination to right past wrongs, to find a quick antidote for history. This renaissance has had wide-ranging consequences. The Civil Rights Movement at long last brought Negro Americans, who were still disfranchised in large parts of the country and were still excluded from many avenues of educational opportunity and political preferment, into the main current of American life. Handicapped persons were treated with a new consideration, and provided everyday conveniences that eased their lives. Prisoners' hopes and frustrations were put in the spotlight. Homosexuality was de-criminalized and homosexuals came to be treated with unprecedented tolerance. Women—the Forgotten Men of American History—were made more the equals of men. Altogether, there was a strenuous effort to give every human being his due.

But all these sensitizings of the American conscience have brought a cautiousness, an unaccustomed intellectual wariness. While Americans talk with a new freedom, certain questions—such as the meaning of intelligence tests, the in-

fluence of poverty on the family and homebred culture—
have tended to be quietly suppressed or openly tabooed. Any
territory on which some minority—racial, religious, ethnic,
sexual, or biological—has posted its no-trespassing signs
becomes a place where career-conscious scholars or scientists
had better tread lightly, and where the prudent politician
dare not tread at all. The well-justified pangs of social conscience become an unjustifiable intellectual timidity, a fear of
exploring. Areas (such as the economics of the institution of
slavery) which have not been properly or impartially treated
by historians, sociologists, psychologists, or political scientists are suddenly pronounced out of bounds. Meanwhile, the
partisan passions of each "minority"—Negroes, women,
homosexuals and others—motivate new literatures of petty
chauvinism. Only the bold scholar, more secure in his liveli-
hood than most, dares become a Negative Explorer.

These, among other forces, have dulled the exploring spirit
and have discouraged any but the most intrepid. Yet, on the
whole, these forces are the ironic by-products of our strenuous efforts to "perfect" democracy in America.

EXPLORING AND DEMOCRACY

At the same time, luckily, twentieth-century America has
produced new sources of the Exploring Spirit, new agencies
of Negative Discovery. Some of these, too, are by-products
of American technology.

The Exploring Press. The traditional role of the daily press
was well stated by the first American journalist in the first
issue of the first newspaper printed in British North Amer-

ica. "It is designed," Benjamin Harris explained in his *Publick Occurrences Both Forreign and Domestick,* which appeared in Boston on September 25, 1690, "that the Countrey shall be furnished once a moneth (or, if any Glut of Occurrences happen, oftener,) with an Account of such considerable things as have arrived unto our Notice." (It is worth noting that this first issue, not having been duly licensed, was quickly suppressed.) A century later, the New York *Evening Post* in its opening issue of November 15, 1801, showed that the newspaper function had hardly changed. "The design of this paper is to diffuse among the people correct information on all interesting subjects, to inculcate just principles in religion, morals, and politics, and to cultivate a taste for sound literature." Newspapers, then, set themselves the task of "reporting," of bringing information to the public.

During the nineteenth century, as weeklies became dailies, as the size of papers increased, as advertising expanded, as readership enlarged into a mass circulation, and as papers competed with one another for the hundreds of thousands of readers, newspapers found it hard to fill their columns only with "such considerable things as have arrived unto our Notice." They had to make news, to prod stories into being, and to create pseudo-events. Enterprising newspapermen personally financed the staging of news—for example, James Gordon Bennett sent Stanley on the African journey to find Livingstone, Joseph Pulitzer sponsored the round-the-world trip of Nellie Bly to beat the eighty-day record of Jules Verne's Phineas Fogg. Newspapers had to make things happen so that they could be reported.

Toward the end of the nineteenth century, a new tradition emerged in the American press. Compounded of conscience, imagination, ambition, and original sin, it was the product of the "Muckrakers." These ran the gamut from serious writers like Ida M. Tarbell and Lincoln Steffens at one end to scores of petty, reckless, self-seeking, self-righteous newspaper gossips at the other. The best of them were explorers. Their service was perhaps less in bringing reliable new information than in awakening the citizenry to vast areas of national life that were still unexplored. While the muckraking journalists made their money and their reputations as discoverers, turning up what they knew in advance must be there, their enduring place in American life would be as explorers. They, too, pointed to dark continents.

Their descendants in our time are the so-called "investigative reporters." These helped awaken the nation to the Watergate Scandals, and since then have opened the way to many obscure islands of national life. Their service, too, is less as messengers of fact than as watchmen in the night, alerting us to the limits of our knowledge. As our government becomes bigger and more powerful, armed with a technology against which the individual citizen feels powerless, the exploring press has become more than ever indispensable to a free society.

The Exploring Congress. The tripartite division of powers on which the Founding Fathers framed the Constitution provided a legislature to make the laws, an executive to enforce the laws, and a judiciary to interpret the laws. In the twentieth century, the Congress has taken on itself the additional role of Public Explorer. Congressional investigating committees have become bold explorers—pointers toward dark continents of the national life. They open the eyes of the citizenry to subjects which the executive has no motive to explore (or may have motives to keep secret), and which the press has not the powers to explore. They have touched everything—from immigration, labor unions, organized crime, voting rights, law enforcement, to foods and drugs, alcoholic beverages, Watergate, and even the CIA. Hardly a corner of our national life has been left unexplored. This Congressional power-to-explore is, for all practical purposes, unlimited. The opportunity for abuse of the individual citizen is great, and, in the hands of a Senator Joe McCarthy, can wreak havoc on the lives of innocents. The temptations to posturing and demagoguery grow every year with the stage-managing of Congressional hearings into television spectaculars.

But in spite of their abuses, Congressional investigating committees have come to play a role for us Americans which the medieval chancellor played for his monarch. They are the keepers of our public conscience. And they become a modern hallmark of our free society. While governments in most of the world scheme to secrete their acts from their citizens, these new American agencies are the enemies of secrecy. While other forms of government remain messy underneath, democracy prefers to be messy on the surface. Our Congress has taken on the duty to see that the mess is not submerged, and so constantly to remind the citizenry of how much they still don't know.

The Skeptical Layman. While the Exploring Press and the Exploring Congress are both in many ways by-products of technology, the American layman himself is an antidote to technology. He can ensure that we are not overwhelmed by what technology has done to us, nor overimpressed by our ability to predict technology's future course. As a nonexpert, who has *not* spent years becoming at home in the jargon of some specialty, the layman has no vested interest in the state of any science at this particular moment. He is no more at home in today's technical jargon than in yesterday's or tomorrow's. The layman has no reason *not* to believe in the obsolescence of expertise. Therefore he is freer than the expert in his hopes and his expectations. He is the ombudsman of the impossible.

In *Profiles of the Future,* Arthur C. Clarke shows us how experts are tempted to fence us back from the future. The self-respect of their profession sometimes actually requires them to do so. There is hardly a major technological achievement of our time—including the splitting of the atom and the voyage to the moon—which the experts of the last generation did not solemnly pronounce to be impossible. Clarke rightly concludes that when an expert (especially an aged and distinguished one) tells us that something can't be done, we must not believe him. The only person who can save us from these specious (if eminently respectable) impossibilities is the layman. He alone does not know enough to dogmatize about the impossible. The community of laymen keeps wide open our windows to the future, our vistas of the otherwise.

According to the conventional wisdom, the masses of the people are weak in imagination, slow to accept novelty, reluctant to move out of old ruts, and hence are those who man the barricades against progress. They will not accept anything new, we are told, except as a last resort. Even if this notion does sum up the experience of aristocratic Old World societies, where the masses were a phlegmatic rooted peasantry or a miserable urban mob, it is the opposite of the truth in the United States. Marxist stereotypes of urban proletariat and rural bumpkins—the "workers and peasants" of Bolshevik slogans—may have been a useful caricature of Old World society, but they have nothing to do with us. Twenty years after the American people discovered the automobile, it had become a daily necessity for nearly everybody; twenty years after the first commercial television set went on the market, nearly every American had adopted it into his living room. Of course, American wealth and technology have helped make this possible. Old World nations, following American example, and sometimes with American know-how, have shown a new hospitality to innovation, and have embraced the automobile and television with an almost American haste. But American wealth and technology themselves have been a by-product of the willingness of a democratic people to accept the new. Perhaps the most important novelty which American experience has opened to the social science of the world is this simple revelation: that a vast literate populace can be hospitable to, even eager for, all sorts of novelty.

The democratic citizenry of a technologically triumphant America have learned calmly to take for granted everyday violations of yesterday's common sense. We have seen too many common-sense axioms go with the wind. The common citizen, the proverbial bulwark of common sense, has become the most enthusiastic greeter of its daily nullification. We are not shocked in the United States when colored motion pictures fly thousands of miles through thick walls to reach each of us instantaneously, or when our climate is controlled, or when the human heart is repaired or replaced. In exploring the invisible atom, we have taken less persuading than Ferdinand and Isabella required, and we invest a thousandfold what they invested. While we lay Americans have lost some of our wholesome sense of wonder, we no longer see an opaque wall separating us from the impossible.

We become skeptical, not only of what science can do, but of what newsmen can tell us. It was some years ago that Will Rogers could say, "All I know is what I see in the papers." Nowadays, a literate, overexposed public gains a new capacity for boredom and for skepticism. The defeat of Senator Joe McCarthy was finally accomplished not by confining him among bureaucrats and experts, but by giving him the widest television exposure. The skeptical layman had had too much of him.

Multiplying specializations and expanding expertise have given the layman a necessary new role. The more professionalized our knowledge becomes, the more we need the skeptical spirit of the layman. However unwittingly, he has become the catalyst for the exploring spirit. Democracy was once best described as a government by the common people. Now, perhaps, we should begin to think of it as a government by laymen.

What finally are the widest openings that American civilization has helped provide for the vision of all mankind? Perhaps the greatest American opening has been toward boundless new vistas of the unknown and the unpredictable. The most important American addition to the World Experience was the simple surprising fact of America.

We have helped prepare mankind for all its later surprises. America has invigorated the whole human quest for openings, and has provided new energy and new resources for that quest. We are a source of faith, hope and charity for all who share the exploring enterprise.

In the earliest era of American history—the Founding Era —the Exploring Spirit flourished from the peculiar opportunities, the wealth, and even the poverties, of the American landscape. These were a free gift to the peoples of the Old World, if not provided by God, surely not manufactured by man. In our age, an age when our most intimate environment is not the Land but the Machine, *we* make both the landscape of exploring and the vehicles of exploration. We have become both the explorers and the explored.

ACKNOWLEDGMENTS

This book is a revision of the Reith Lectures which I recorded for the BBC at Broadcasting House in London during the week of October 23, 1975, and which were broadcast on BBC radio weekly beginning on November 12, 1975. I want to thank the governors of the British Broadcasting Corporation for the opportunity to deliver these lectures to an audience in the country which I consider my second home, for the incentive they have given me to bring these thoughts together, and for their delightful hospitality to my wife and me during our week in London. I want especially to thank my friends George Fischer and Philip French for their patience, wise advice and guidance.

Readers of my earlier books, *The Americans: The Colonial Experience* (Random House, 1958) and *The Image: A Guide to Pseudo-Events in America* (Atheneum, 1961), will find that I have drawn from those books a few examples for new purposes.

This book, like all my others, owes more than I can explain to my wife, Ruth F. Boorstin, who has not only made it possible, but has made the quest for these ideas and for their precise statement a happy voyage of exploring in tandem.

ABOUT THE AUTHOR

DANIEL J. BOORSTIN, the Librarian of Congress, was senior historian of the Smithsonian Institution, Washington, D.C., and director of the National Museum of History and Technology from 1969 to 1973. Until 1969, he was Preston and Sterling Morton Distinguished Service Professor of American History at the University of Chicago, where he taught for twenty-five years.

Dr. Boorstin has spent a good deal of his life viewing America from the outside, first in England, where he was a Rhodes Scholar at Balliol College, Oxford, winning a coveted "double-first," and was admitted as a barrister-at-law of the Inner Temple, London. More recently he has been visiting professor of American History at the University of Rome and at Kyoto University, consultant to the Social Science Research Center at the University of Puerto Rico, the first incumbent of the chair of American History at the Sorbonne, and Pitt Professor of American History and Institutions and a Fellow of Trinity College, Cambridge University, which awarded him its Litt.D. degree.

Born in Georgia in 1914 and raised in Oklahoma, Dr. Boorstin received his B.A. with highest honors from Harvard and his doctor's degree from Yale. He is a member of the Massachusetts Bar and has practiced law. Before going to Chicago in 1944, he taught at Harvard and Swarthmore. He has lectured widely within this country and all over the world.

The Americans, his most extensive work, is a trilogy with a sweeping new view of American history, revealing through the story of our past some of the secrets of the distinctive character of

American culture. The third volume, *The Americans: The Democratic Experience* (1973), was a main selection of the Book-of-the-Month Club and won the Pulitzer Prize. Dr. Boorstin has received several other awards, including the Bancroft Prize for *The Americans: The Colonial Experience* (1958) and the Francis Parkman Prize for *The Americans: The National Experience* (1965).

Among his other books are *The Image: A Guide to Pseudo-Events in America* (1964, 1971), *The Genius of American Politics* (1953), *The Decline of Radicalism* (1969), and *Democracy and Its Discontents.* The editor of the twenty-seven-volume *Chicago History of American Civilization* series, he is also the author of a television show and of numerous popular articles and books.

Dr. Boorstin is married to the former Ruth Frankel, and the Boorstins have three sons.